TAKE-HOME BOOKS

Harcourt Brace & Company

Orlando   Atlanta   Austin   Boston   San Francisco   Chicago   Dallas   New York   Toronto   London

ISBN 0-15-307476-0

1 2 3 4 5 6 7 8 9 10 022 99 98 97 96

CONTENTS

HORSES AND RIDERS

by Paul Fehlner

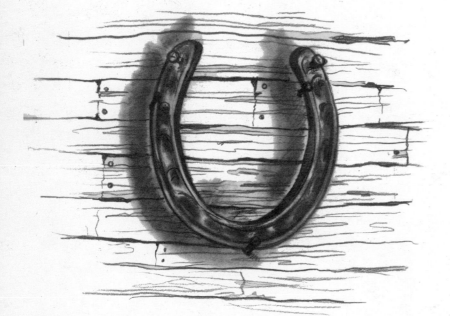

HARCOURT BRACE & COMPANY

Great American Horses

The Appaloosa is a spotted or speckled horse from the American West. It was a favorite of Native Americans.

The Morgan horse is skillful at racing and jumping.

The palomino has a golden coat, dark eyes, and a white or ivory mane and tail.

The pinto has large white and dark patches.

The quarter horse is a strong, fast horse developed to run quarter-mile races. Quarter horses now often work on ranches.

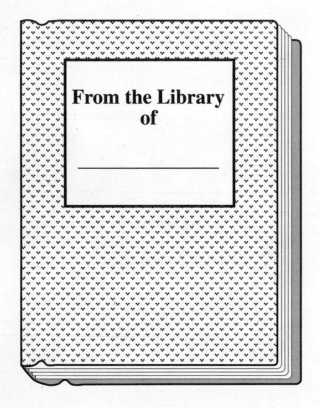

From the Library of
_____

Pinto

Appaloosa

Quarter horse

Morgan

Palamino

European explorers brought horses to the Americas hundreds of years ago. Some of these horses got away from the explorers. These horses scattered throughout the West. The pioneer settlers called these wild horses *mustangs.*

At one time, thousands of mustangs ran across the plains. They lived in groups called *bands.* One male horse, called a *stallion,* accompanied each band.

As people moved west, they found that mustangs caused problems. The mustangs ate grass, so cattle ranchers drove them off their grazing lands. They also ate crops, so farmers drove them off their farms.

Today, very few mustangs are left in the wild. But some people are working to save the few that are left. They seem to stand for the things people love about horses. They are strong, smart, wild, and free.

People often say that a dog is man's best friend. But horses have also been very helpful to people for thousands of years.

Long before there were any cars, trains, or planes, horses helped people get from place to place. Horses pulled wagons and stagecoaches. They carried soldiers and even helped deliver the mail. Horses pulled streetcars in America's cities. Horses helped farmers plow their fields for planting.

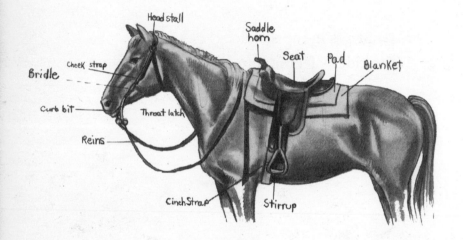

Head stall
Saddle horn
Seat
Pad
Blanket
Bridle
Cheek strap
Curb bit
Throat latch
Reins
Cinch Strap
Stirrup

Today, horses are most often used for fun. People ride for pleasure through parks and on beaches. Horses perform at the circus. Riders show their skill at rodeos and in horse shows.

People put special items on the horse before they ride it. The items are called *tack*. Tack for riding includes the bridle, the saddle, a saddle pad, and a blanket. Straps around the horse's middle hold the saddle in place.

The largest horses are called *draft horses*. They were used on farms and in logging camps. People have used draft horses to pull plows, heavy wagons, and other loads.

Hundreds of years ago, big draft horses, such as the Clydesdale, carried knights in armor. Only a very strong horse could carry all that weight!

Today, machines do the work draft horses used to do. But some draft horses do still work on farms.

Shetland Pony

The smallest horses are called *ponies*. They may be only three or four feet tall. The very smallest pony is called the Shetland pony.

Ponies are strong. People once used ponies to pull carts through narrow mine tunnels. Today, ponies might carry riders on narrow mountain trails. Young children like to ride them at street fairs or at zoos.

Ponies are just right for children who are learning to ride but are too small for a full-size horse.

A rider gets on a horse from the left side. The rider straddles, or puts one leg on each side of, the horse and sits in the saddle.

The rider's feet fit into stirrups that hang from the saddle. The rider holds on to the reins. Reins are thin straps that are attached to the bridle around the horse's head. Moving the reins gives the horse messages about which way to go.

On long rides, horses have to take breaks so they can eat. Horses need to eat a lot of food. They usually eat grain and hay. In warm weather, horses may graze in grassy meadows. They also need a lot of water.

Horses love apples or carrot treats! Usually, the rider feeds a horse these treats by hand. If you feed a horse, you should hold your hand flat. Have the food in your palm. When the horse whinnies, it usually means the horse is happy with the treat.

Thoroughbred horses have more slender legs than other kinds of horses. They are very fast. Most race horses are thoroughbreds.

There are many farms in Kentucky where thoroughbreds are raised. Kentucky is the home of the Kentucky Derby. The Kentucky Derby is a famous race that is run every May.

The best-known thoroughbred from the United States was named Man O' War. Out of 21 races, he lost only one!

Man O' War

Horses live in stables. There, each horse has its own small area, called a *stall*. Horses rest there and eat there.

Most horses do not like to be alone for very long, though. They would rather stay together in a group. Watch horses that are grazing in a meadow. They will probably stay quite close to each other.

Horses that are bred to race are not as calm as most other horses. Sometimes they get nervous. When that happens, they may fight each other. They may bite or kick. You should not go near a horse if you have not learned how to handle one.

Horses that most people ride are called *light horses.* Their legs are rather thin. They do not weigh as much as horses that are used to do heavy work.

The Arabian horse is one type of light horse. It is small, but strong. Arabian horses first lived in the desert.

Many other kinds of horses are related to the Arabian horse. One of these is the thoroughbred.

All horses need plenty of exercise. One way for a horse to get exercise is to run at a gallop in a meadow. Another is to be ridden by a person.

Sometimes, a trainer has the horse run in circles on a long leash. This leash is called a *longe line* [löng līne].

While the horse runs, the training goes on. The horse learns to follow commands. It learns to start and stop. It learns to go faster or slower. Horses go through this training even before they carry a rider on their backs.

This horse is wearing its bridle and saddle. It is ready to ride.

Good riders sit up straight in the saddle. They talk to the horse with their voices. They also give messages with their legs and hands.

Leg movements tell the horse to move left or right. Hand and leg signals together tell the horse to go faster or to stop. The rider can also lean his or her body to tell a horse to start, stop, or turn.

Harcourt Brace School Publishers

TAKE-HOME BOOK

The Orphan

by Sharon Fear

HARCOURT BRACE & COMPANY

From the
Library
of

"Will you keep it?" asked Randy.

"No. Wild animals don't make good pets."

But when his uncle saw the look on Randy's face, he said, "We'll let it go right here on the farm. But not until it's strong. Until then, you'll have to come back and visit often. You can help us bring it up. Would you like that?"

"Oh, yes," said Randy.

"Chrrrt," said the woodchuck.

Randy walked to the end of the driveway. Cars went by on the highway. One, two, then two more. "They're going to the fair," Randy said to himself. "Me too. . . maybe."

Every year, he came to stay with his aunt and uncle so he could go to the county fair. And every year it was the same thing. He was dressed! He was ready! But no one else was.

"Come on! Come on!" he sang as he hopped up and down.

Then he heard something. He thought he heard a tiny cry. He stopped hopping and listened. There! He heard it again. He followed the sound down into the ditch. And there was a little animal. It was not much bigger than his two hands when he reached for it.

Wait. Maybe he shouldn't pick it up. He might hurt it. Or it might hurt him. He didn't know what to do.

When Randy's alarm rang, he got up and went to the kitchen. He looked at the woodchuck. Fast asleep. Then he checked his list and went carefully through the steps. While he was feeding the baby, his uncle came in and sat down to watch.

"Let's see if it likes to be petted," said Uncle Steve. He rubbed the back of the woodchuck's neck very gently.

The little woodchuck stopped eating. "Chrrrt. . . chrrrt," it said.

2

11

They told Uncle Steve about the orphan. "Uh, oh," he said. "Three-hour feedings."

"You two go on," Aunt May said. "I'll stay."

"I'll stay," said Randy. His aunt and uncle looked surprised. "Really," he said. "I want to."

"Well," said his uncle, "let's all stay home. The rodeo is tomorrow night, anyway. And that's our favorite part of the fair. Right, Randy?"

"And I'll stay home tomorrow," said Aunt May.

"No, I will," said Uncle Steve.

"I will," said Randy.

They all laughed. "Let's decide tomorrow," said Uncle Steve.

Aunt May would know.

"Aunt May!" He ran in the back door, letting the screen door slam. "Whoa!" said his aunt. "Always in such a hurry!"

"There's a baby animal in the ditch. It may be hurt. Come and look. Please."

"We'll need this," she said, taking a towel from the stack on the dryer.

"It's a baby woodchuck," said Aunt May. "You were right to call me, Randy. Never touch a strange animal, wild or tame." The woodchuck was a fat, furry little thing with a short, bushy tail. Its eyes were shut.

"We mustn't pick it up if it's not really lost," said his aunt. "Look around for its mother."

Randy walked a little way along the ditch. Suddenly, he stopped. Up ahead, near the road, was an adult woodchuck. Dead. Hit by a car, he guessed.

When he told his aunt, she gently picked up the little woodchuck in the towel. They took it to the house.

"Well. . . okay," said Aunt May. "But there's a lot to do. Let's go wash our hands. Then we'll make a list."

So, as his aunt told him what to do, Randy wrote it all down.

1. Set alarm.
2. Check heating pad.
3. Warm milk.
4. Feed two teaspoons. No more!
5. Wash medicine dropper in hot water, soap, and bleach.
6. Wash hands in bathroom.
7. Set alarm for three hours.

Aunt May was satisfied that Randy understood what to do. Just then his uncle Steve came in the back door. "Everybody ready?" he asked.

Aunt May and Randy looked at each other. "The fair," said Randy. "I forgot."

4

9

In no time Randy was confidently feeding the little woodchuck. It even opened its eyes and looked at Randy. But before it drank all its milk, the woodchuck's eyes closed and its little head nodded.

"Is it okay?" Randy asked, worried.

"It's just fallen asleep," said Aunt May. They put it back in the warm bed and checked the heating pad.

"It will have to be fed every three hours, day and night, for a while," said Aunt May.

Randy was reluctant to ask, but. . . "May I do it? I can feed him. I watched everything you did. I could set my alarm . . . "

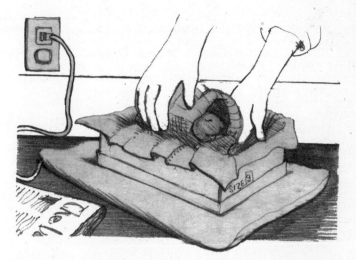

"Is it alive?" asked Randy.

"Yes," said Aunt May. "But it's cold and weak. Let's warm it up."

Aunt May got the heating pad, plugged it in, and turned it on low. Then she got an empty box and set it on top of the pad.

"Never put a heating pad in the box with the baby," she said. "It can get too hot."

She put another towel inside the box. Then she put the baby woodchuck, still snug in his towel, in the box. Finally, she covered the box with some newspaper. She left a corner open for fresh air.

"While it's warming up, we'll make it some baby food. Randy, get me that little pan behind the skillets there." Aunt May put a cup of milk into the pan to heat. Then she added a tablespoon of corn syrup.

"Don't boil the milk. Just heat it until you see little bubbles around the edge. If I don't have corn syrup, I use honey. Now," she said, turning off the heat, "let the milk cool till it's just barely warm."

While the milk cooled, she looked through a drawer full of utensils until she found a medicine dropper. She washed it in hot, soapy water with a little bleach in it.

"If you handle the baby, wash your hands. Wild animals can have diseases. Wash them in the bathroom, not in the kitchen!"

"Yes, Ma'am," he answered. He could see she was serious.

When the milk was cool enough, she put some in the dropper.

"We'll feed it about two teaspoons at a time," she said.

She picked up the baby in his towel. She put the dropper to it mouth and squeezed out one drop. Its mouth opened.

"It likes that!" said Randy.

"It's your turn," said Aunt May.

Randy was suddenly scared. "I can't," he said. "I don't know how!"

"Just do what I did," said Aunt May. She handed him the baby wrapped in his towel.

6

7

TAKE-HOME BOOK

Eliza's Circus

by Susan McCloskey

HARCOURT BRACE & COMPANY

From the
Library
of

_____

And that was how Eliza Abbot, farm girl, became Mademoiselle Eliza, circus performer! It was a dream come true! (And Pierette had a good time, too.)

"Eliza! Eliza!" called Mrs. Abbot. "Where could that girl be? I haven't seen her since breakfast."

"Well, she could be doing her chores," said Mr. Abbot. "But she's probably behind the barn, trying to teach the dogs to walk like people."

Mrs. Abbot sighed. She wondered what had happened to the sweet Eliza she knew. She did her chores and helped her parents . . . where had this new Eliza come from? This girl had nothing but silly ideas about teaching dogs to do tricks.

"It's all my fault," Mrs. Abbot said. She shook her head. "I wish I'd never taken her to that circus. She's been in a trance ever since."

12

1

It was true. Eliza's visit to the circus last month had changed her. She had laughed as the jugglers tossed plates high in the air. She had screeched as the acrobats flipped across the ring. She had gasped as the trapeze artists flew through the air like birds. But one act had enchanted her more than all the others.

A tall woman led her fluffy white poodles into the ring.

"Introducing—Madame Fifi and her Trained Poodles!" boomed the ringmaster.

Madame Fifi soon cleared up the mystery. She told them that the circus train had derailed some months before. Many of the animals had run away in fear, but they had all been found. All except Pierette.

"I left the circus early to come back and look for her," Madame Fifi explained. "You have taken such good care of her! And Mr. Lopez tells me you have taught her a new trick. How can I ever thank you for keeping her safe?"

Suddenly, Eliza knew just how she wanted to be thanked.

"Make me your protégée!" she cried.

2

11

Before long, Mr. Lopez returned. With him, in a pink dressing gown, was Madame Fifi!

As soon as Bette saw Madame Fifi, she gave a sharp bark. She jumped out the window of the automobile. Then she ran toward the famous trainer as fast as she could go.

"Pierette! My darling!" cried Madame Fifi. "Where have you been? I have been frantic with worry!"

Eliza almost fainted with surprise.

Madame Fifi's smile never dimmed. She commanded her dogs to do wonderful tricks. One balanced a ball on his nose and waved his paws in the air. One jumped through a ring. Another somersaulted over a jump rope held by two other dogs.

Eliza had never seen such creatures. The only dogs she knew were gruff, hard-working farm dogs. They were nothing like the fluffy poodles that twirled in the ring.

Eliza could not get Madame Fifi out of her mind. Instead of doing chores, she sat and daydreamed. She imagined she was in the circus, with dogs of her own.

For weeks she practiced on the farm dogs. She sewed big collars for them. She hoped the collars made them look like poodles. Then she tried to teach them to walk on their back legs like Madame Fifi's

The very next day, Mr. Lopez drove the Abbots and Bette into the city. They threaded their way through the crowded streets. Finally, they pulled up in front of an old house. It had a sign that said *Seaside Boardinghouse*.

"Wait right here," said Mr. Lopez. "I'll bring Madame Fifi down."

Eliza could hardly wait to meet Madame Fifi. Neither could Bette, it seemed. She squirmed and whined as she stared at the boardinghouse.

A few weeks later, a man was driving by. He was amazed to see a shaggy white dog standing on the back of a trotting horse. He stopped and talked to Eliza.

"My name is Mr. Lopez. I'm an agent for the circus. That's a good trick you've got there. I think that Madame Fifi might be interested in it. Would you and your dog like to meet her?"

Eliza could scarcely believe her ears. She was going to meet Madame Fifi!

8

Peppy the collie was a willing student. He let Eliza hold his front paws and walk around in a circle. But just when he seemed ready to walk by himself, one of the sheep trotted by.

Off ran Peppy.

"These dogs are meant to work, not prance around in fancy collars," Eliza's father reminded her. By then, Peppy's collar was torn and muddy and not at all fancy. But Eliza knew her father was right.

5

Early the next morning, Eliza stepped outside to do her chores. There at the bottom of the steps was a most unhappy-looking dog. She whined with hunger. Her white fur was caked with mud and covered with burrs. But Eliza wanted her for her very own.

"Let her keep the dog," Mr. Abbot told his wife. "Eliza can teach *her* tricks. Then maybe she'll stop bothering the other dogs."

Eliza named her new dog Bette.

It seemed Bette was born to do tricks. She enjoyed walking on her back legs and waving her front paws in the air. Mr. and Mrs. Abbot were astonished! Bette loved to turn somersaults. She could even walk along the top of the fence without wavering . . . just like a tightrope walker!

Mr. and Mrs. Abbot applauded. Eliza and Bette bowed. But Eliza knew these tricks were nothing compared to the one she had in mind.

6

7

TAKE-HOME BOOK

Fish Friends

by Molly Bridger

HARCOURT BRACE & COMPANY

Try This!

Here are some Japanese words that Luke's new friend might teach him. Try saying them aloud.

ichi	[ee´chi]	=	=	one
ni	[nee]	=	=	two
san	[sahn]	=	=	three
hi	[hee]	=	=	day/sun
getsu	[get´soo]	=	=	month/ moon
yama	[yah´mah]	=	=	mountain
kawa	[kah´wah]	=	=	river
tomodachi	[toh•moh•da´chee]	=	=	friend

"Thank you," Luke said as he took the bag. He scattered more food on the pond for the fish. As he did, it he whispered thank you to the fish, too.

Then, while the fish gobbled up their snack, Luke and his new companion went off to play baseball together.

"Japan!" Luke exclaimed. "We have to go to Japan?"

"We'll have a wonderful time," Mom said.

"It's only for six months," Dad said.

Six months. Luke looked around his bedroom. He loved this room. He loved his books and his baseball card collection. He looked at his goldfish. He thought about the kids in his class and on his baseball team.

"I can't leave!" Luke said. "What about baseball? What about Swish and Fin and all my friends?"

"You can bring your baseball cards along," Dad said, "But your fish and your friends will have to stay here."

"You'll make new friends," Mom said. "It will be great fun."

But it wasn't fun. It wasn't fun at all. In Japan, Luke's mom and dad worked most of the time. He went to school.

School was okay. At least people there spoke English. But it was the middle of the year. Everyone else had already made friends.

The other kids came from all over the world. No one played baseball. The school was big and spread out. They went to different rooms for each class. Luke kept getting lost.

"The school rambles all over the place," he complained to his mother. "I'm always late to class."

"Ask a friend for help," his mom replied.

Luke didn't have a friend. He felt abandoned.

The boy replied. Even though he spoke in Japanese, Luke knew what he meant. He could borrow a glove.

"Okay! I'm ready," Luke said, jumping off the bench. "Let's go!"

But first the boy held up the paper bag. He took a pinch of stuff from inside and sprinkled it in the pond. The fish gulped it up.

Then the boy offered the bag to Luke.

Luke couldn't believe it. His new friend liked baseball *and* fish. Maybe he liked baseball cards, too.

The boy nodded his head.

"*Beisu boru*," he repeated. He pointed to the far side of the park.

Luke looked. He saw lots of kids over there. Some were tossing balls back and forth. A couple were swinging bats. A few were stretching.

The boy pointed at them. Then he pointed at Luke. He spoke so quickly that Luke couldn't tell where one word ended and the next one began. But Luke didn't need a translation. The boy wanted Luke to play, too.

"I don't have a glove," Luke said, holding up his bare hand.

At first, Luke spent a lot of time in his new bedroom.

It was different from his room at home. The floor had mats made out of straw. His bed, called a futon, was like a mattress on the floor.

Luke had space to sort baseball cards. Without a friend, though, baseball cards weren't much fun.

Every afternoon after school, Luke threw himself on his futon and dreamed about home. He missed his best friend, Mark. He missed his goldfish, too. Without Swish and Fin, he didn't have anyone to complain to.

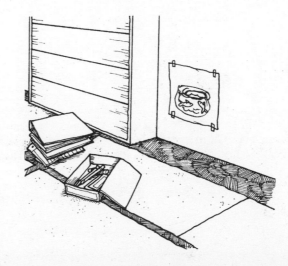

After a while, staying in his room got boring. Even though he didn't know how to talk to people, Luke went for long walks around his new town.

There was so much to see. The signs were in a different language, with different letters. People wore different kinds of shoes on their feet. Even the dogs looked different. Luke couldn't recognize many of the breeds.

He passed people who smiled at him. Some even talked to him, but he couldn't understand what they said.

Luke looked up. A boy was sitting on the other end of the bench. He had a baseball hat on his head. He was holding a baseball glove and a bat. He was holding a paper bag, too.

"Baseball!" Luke said. "Do you play?" He pointed at the boy, then swung a pretend bat to make sure he understood.

"I'm sure bean paste ice cream is very good, if that is what you expect." Luke sighed.

He thought about other things he missed.

"I miss all my friends. I miss crawling under my bed and looking for lost socks. I miss sticking posters on my wall. But most of all, aside from friends, I miss baseball. . . "

"*Beisu boru?*"

Once he bumped into a lady. She smiled and she looked so kind!

Luke said, "Excuse me."

To himself, he pretended that she was his first new friend. Maybe she was the wife of the most famous baseball player in Japan. She would introduce them, and they would go to all the games.

But the lady just bowed and said something Luke could not understand. She was just one of many passersby.

"I wish I had somebody to talk to," Luke said out loud. Nobody answered.

One day, Luke found a small park near his house. It had benches and paths. It also had a pool, and the pool was full of fish.

Luke sat down on a bench by the pool.

"Hi," he said to the fish.

The fish didn't say anything back. But Luke felt they were listening to him, just like Fin and Swish.

"You remind me of my fish at home," he said.

The fish glided around in the pool. One swam to the top of the water. It opened its mouth. Then it dove down again.

"Swish and Fin do that, too," Luke told the fish. "I miss them. Mark is taking care of them for me."

The fish swam close to the edge of the pool.

"I miss Mark," Luke said. "I miss my whole fourth grade class." He leaned over the pool.

"Do you know I can't even get my favorite ice cream here? The other day, Dad bought me some ice cream. He thought it was chocolate. I like chocolate best. But it wasn't chocolate. It was bean paste. Bean paste ice cream!"

The fish swam around calmly.

TAKE-HOME BOOK

HARCOURT BRACE & COMPANY

Guide Dog Heros

by Paul Fehlner

From the
Library
of

More About Guide Dogs

State and Federal laws let guide dogs go anywhere. They can even go into grocery stores and onto airplanes.

If you see a person with a guide dog, do not get in the way. Never touch a guide dog's harness. Do not feed the dog.

If you'd like a comic book story called *The Story of Bonny, A Seeing Eye Dog* write to:

The Seeing Eye, Inc.
Post Office Box 375
Morristown, New Jersey 07963-0375

Remember Morris Frank and Buddy? One day they were leaving an office. They headed for the elevator. Suddenly Buddy stopped. He refused to budge.

Morris tried to force Buddy to keep walking. He thought the dog was afraid of the elevator. Buddy stayed still.

Then a horrified woman came over. She told Morris that Buddy had saved his life. The elevator door had opened on an empty elevator shaft!

Guide dogs don't spend all their time being heroes. At home, they can just relax and be loving companions.

Isn't it wonderful how guide dogs help their masters in so many ways?

Everybody knows that dogs make good pets. But did you know that dogs also work?

Dogs herd cattle and sheep. Dogs search for people who are lost. Police dogs help catch criminals. They also find victims of earthquakes and avalanches. These dogs have rescued people who are unconscious.

Guide dogs are a very special group of working dogs. They are trained to help blind people.

Golden Retriever Labrador Retriever

The first guide dogs helped people who were blinded in World War I. The idea to train them originated in Germany. Soon other countries began to train guide dogs, too.

A young man from Nashville, Tennessee, heard about the guide dogs. His name was Morris Frank. Morris had been blind since he was a boy. He thought it would be wonderful to have a guide dog. In fact, he traveled all the way to Switzerland to get one!

One of the hardest skills the guide dog learns is to stay calm in a crowd. There may be many people around when its master goes to work or goes shopping. Some dogs feel as if they're going to suffocate among so many people. A guide dog must not panic.

Guide dogs also have to learn to ignore other dogs, squirrels, birds, and even cats. And they cannot stop for people who want to pet them.

Sometimes guide dogs disobey on purpose! For example, a guide dog is trained not to step into the street if a car is coming. The dog must also ignore a "Forward" command if something blocks the way.

But the training isn't over! Next, the dog and student begin to train together. It is hard for most students to follow a dog's lead. This is a new feeling.

The dog stops suddenly. It sees a fallen tree branch in the way. But the student does not see it. She wonders why the dog has stopped. She doesn't know until the dog leads her around the branch. Leaves brush the student's leg. Then she understands.

At first, a trainer goes everywhere with the guide dog and the student. The trainer helps the dog learn to obey commands. One important command is "fetch." At first, the dog fetches a toy or a ball. Later, it will learn to get all sorts of things that its owner needs.

10

German Shepherd

Morris returned home with Buddy, a German shepherd. Buddy was the first trained guide dog in America.

Morris and Buddy traveled all over the country. Morris talked to people about guide dogs. Soon, many other Americans had them, too.

Most guide dogs are German shepherds, golden retrievers, or Labrador retrievers. Each of these kinds of dogs has the right instincts for guide dog work.

Guide dogs must be friendly. They cannot be afraid of loud noises or new places. They need to be the right size, too. Think how hard it would be for a toy poodle to guide a six-foot-tall man! Guide dogs must be large enough to lead an adult. But they cannot be too large. They may have to squeeze under a seat in a bus, train, or airplane.

3

Guide-dog training starts when a dog is very young. A volunteer family raises the puppy. Before long, it is a member of the family.

During this time, the puppy learns to walk on a leash, sit, stay, and sleep in the house. The family makes sure the puppy is used to a lot of people and noise. Someday it may have to stay calm in a large crowd.

A puppy's life isn't all work. There is also lots of play. A bright, young Labrador retriever may patrol in the yard or chase a butterfly. After all, it is still a puppy!

Finally, the day comes when the dog and a the student are both ready. Then it is time for them to meet each other.

The first meeting is usually a happy time. The dogs feel warmth and love. The students know that soon they will "see" through their guide dog's eyes.

The dogs are not the only ones who need to learn. Their new owners also have to go to school. A teacher works with each new human student. The teacher holds one end of the harness. The student holds the handle. Then the teacher leads the student around, just as a guide dog would.

The teachers study each new student. Is this person rough or gentle? Does the student speak loudly or softly? Does he or she move quickly or slowly? The teacher tries to match each student with just the right dog. Some dogs like gentle people better. Other dogs like quick, forceful people.

A guide dog pup stays with its first family for about 18 months. Then it must leave for a training center.

The training center is a school for dogs. There, the teachers are called trainers. They teach the dogs how to be guides.

The dog lives in a kennel with other dogs in the training program. Now the days of puppy fun and games are over. Real work begins.

The dogs are ready. They already know basic commands, like "sit" and "lie down." They want to work hard. Pleasing the trainer is the best reward for these dogs.

Guide dogs wear a special harness. It connects the dog to its master. The harness has a handle that is easy for a person to grip. The handle is light and is made of leather. It is held onto the dog's harness by straps.

A leash and collar help the trainer control the dog. The trainer never uses the harness for punishment. Each dog owner will learn this lesson, too. The best way to train a guide dog is to praise it whenever possible.

Each dog learns the skills that will let it "see" for a blind person. Training lasts four months.

It takes a lot of talent to be a good guide dog. The dogs learn to pause at curbs and stairs. They learn to go around objects, so the people they are leading won't stumble. They also learn how to guide people across busy streets.

The dogs have to look for more than just danger on the ground. They have to look out for things like ladders, too.

At first, the dogs make many mistakes. For example, a dog may jump over an object on a sidewalk instead of going around it. But it soon learns to guide correctly.

TAKE-HOME BOOK

My Princess

by Billy Aronson

HARCOURT BRACE & COMPANY

From the
Library
of

I don't have much time for humans these days. (Bibbit and I have a few hundred tadpoles of our own to look after.) The girl is still my friend, but it's Bibbit who really matters.

Isn't it funny how things work out? The heroine of my opera turned out to be the heroine of my life!

Years ago, I was very lonely.

I lived with hundreds of uncles, aunts, brothers, sisters, and cousins. There were lots of frogs to play with.

So, why did I feel lonely? Because there was someone special I wanted to get to know. Someone who didn't even know I was alive.

I wanted to be friends with this special someone. But it wasn't going to be easy. She was *very* different from me. She was a human being.

From the first time I saw this girl I liked her. I don't know why! Maybe it was her curly hair. Maybe it was her crooked smile.

Every afternoon she walked right by the pond. But she never even noticed me.

I really wanted to be her friend. I just didn't know how to tell her!

The girl didn't run away. She didn't budge. Instead, she reached down and petted my back!

She *had* understood. She wanted to be my friend, too.

"I'm happy for you," said Bibbit. Bibbit was one great friend.

Now the girl comes to the pond quite often. Sometimes I tell frog jokes. Sometimes, Bibbit and I sing frog songs together.

Bibbit and I have fun singing, hopping, playing, and swimming together.

Just then, I felt a little tug on my shoulder. It was Bibbit. She was smiling. She gave me courage.

I took a deep breath and I began to sing. I was incredible! I sang with power. I leaped with grace. The other frogs could hardly believe it.

They weren't the only ones who noticed. There by the side of the pond, my new human friend was looking right at me— and smiling.

When the show was over, she clapped. I loved the applause. But did she know that I did it all for her? Did she understand that I wanted to be her friend?

I hopped out of the pond, right up to the girl's foot. Then I made a deep bow.

I tried telling her in the morning. I tried telling her at lunch time. I tried telling her in the afternoon. I tried telling her in the evening. But she just didn't understand.

Being understood by a human being can be hard!

Having lots of uncles and aunts is great. When you have a problem, one of them always has an answer.

"Bring her a big, fat fly!" said Aunt Ribbit.

"Paint her a mud picture!" cried Uncle Bugs.

"No, no! Sing her a song!" insisted Uncle Croaker.

Uncle Croaker's idea interested me. My whole family loved to sing. On Friday nights we used to give free concerts.

We also loved telling stories. ("Little Green Riding Hood" and "Sleeping Froggy" were my favorites.)

Maybe I could show this girl how much I liked her by writing. . .

The next time the human girl came to the pond, we all hopped to our places. This was my big chance!

Luckily, the others didn't seem nervous. The toads were great. Boy, were they ugly!

But I was so scared. As the show began I could feel my legs tremble. I was sure I'd sing a wrong note, or fall off a lily pad. What if the girl didn't look at me? What if she just walked away?

I opened my mouth for my first song, but only a squeak came out.

4

9

Her name was Bibbit. She was a little shy, but she agreed to help me out.

Now all the roles were filled, and we got right to work.

Bibbit had a beautiful singing voice! She quickly learned the songs.

A team of volunteers made scenery. The actors learned their lines. We rehearsed and rehearsed.

Finally, we were ready. It was show time!

8

AN OPERA!

I decided to set a story to music to make an opera. That would show the girl that I wanted to be her friend.

First I wrote the music. Then I wrote the story. It was about a human princess who was locked in a castle by some ugly toads. One day a frog prince saw the princess. He wanted to be her friend. But the ugly toads told him to get lost. Of course the frog prince had to be clever to set the princess free.

I named it "The Human Princess."

5

There's another great thing about having lots of aunts and uncles. You always have plenty of actors to audition for parts. I only needed three toads. But my uncles and aunts were *very* good at making ugly faces! So I used all of them.

Aunt Ribbit batted her eyes. Uncle Croaker stuck his tongue out about three feet. Uncle Giggit wrapped his eyelids back around his head. Aunt Ribba–Dibbit swallowed her legs.

Some of my cousins wanted to be in the opera, too. So I let them be the prince's helpers. (All they had to do was follow the prince around and sing "Good idea!" once in a while.)

I would play the prince, of course. But who would be the princess?

Finding someone to play the "Human Princess" was hard. I needed someone with just the right look. None of my relatives looked the least bit human!

So I did something I'd never done before. I hopped over to the next pond.

At first I was worried. The frogs in the other pond looked just as froggy as my own relatives—maybe even froggier!

But then I found her.

She had lime green skin and a wide, rubbery smile. Her eyes were what I noticed first. They were different from other frogs' eyes. They were smaller. They didn't stick out quite as far. They were a little closer together. This girl frog looked just a little bit human.

I'd found just the right frog to play the "Human Princess"!

6

7

Harcourt Brace School Publishers

TAKE-HOME BOOK

THE TOGETHER TEAM

by Janet Craig

HARCOURT BRACE & COMPANY

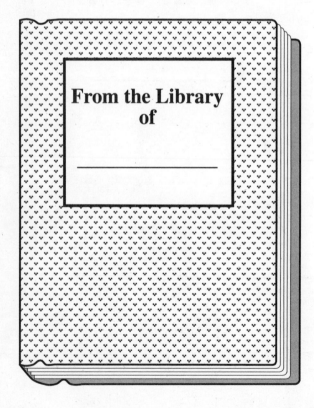

From the Library
of

_____

As I said, I don't know how I let myself get talked into things. But I guess that sometimes it's a good thing that I do.

Sarah has talked me into playing basketball this winter. And I've talked her into joining the History Club.

After all, together we can do just about anything. We're a team!

Sometimes I honestly don't know how I let myself get talked into things.

Take joining the soccer team. We moved to town two months ago. Mom and Dad thought joining a team was a great idea.

They said, "Give it a try, Rosie."

"I don't think so," I said.

"Come on," said Mom. "You'll meet some new friends."

Finally, I said okay. But I didn't really feel okay about it. Sure, I like to kick a soccer ball around with a friend. But I wasn't too sure I wanted to be on a team.

I was even less sure when I showed up for practice. Those kids were good! A lot better than I was. I didn't know any of the players. And because I had missed some of the practices, I didn't know the plays they had already worked out.

Finally, the ball came my way. I got ready to boot it. With all my might, I kicked—and missed it! To top it off, I fell flat on my backside. Talk about humiliations!

Then I saw one of the kids looking at me. There was a grin on her face. Boy, was I mad! Who did she think she was? I quickly got up.

It was during the last game of the season that my big moment came. I was playing defense. The game was tied. There was less than a minute to play. The other team was charging toward our goal.

I got into position. With all my might, I booted the ball straight to Sarah. She took off like a rocket and scored a goal.

Teaching me soccer was another story. But Sarah didn't give up. She showed me how to dribble and pass the ball. And she asked the other kids to include me in the plays.

Our team was pretty good! We even made it to the finals.

I didn't play very hard after that. One thing I did notice. That girl who laughed at me was a great player. She could dribble the ball, pass it, and kick it exactly where she wanted to. Her name was Sarah.

When I got home that afternoon, Mom was working in the study.

"How was practice?" she asked.

"I was completely disgraced!" I said. "And I don't think the other kids liked me. I felt real hostility from them."

"Give them a chance," Mom said. "And give yourself a chance, too."

It was her usual answer.

I had history homework to do. So I got busy. I even forgot about soccer for a while. We were studying about segregation and how people had worked for equal rights. It was pretty interesting.

Our teacher, Mr. Montano, had said we'd be doing something special. Maybe I wasn't a soccer star, but I was a good student. History is my best subject.

The next day, true to his word, Mr. Montano announced, "We're going to be doing some hands-on projects for our unit on equal rights."

We took our time reading the chapter. When it came time to talk about our own ideas about *prejudice,* I said, "I thought you were prejudiced against me at soccer. I thought you didn't like me just because I can't play as well as you can. And because I'm new on the team."

Sarah smiled a little smile. "And I thought *you* didn't like me because I'm not such a great student," she said.

"I guess we were both wrong," I said.

She nodded. "We should get to know somebody before we judge them." Then she said, "Hey, I know what we can do for our project—I'll teach you the plays for soccer. You'll be part of the team in no time. That's a way to fight prejudice, isn't it?"

"Right," I said. "I'll do it—but only if you promise to meet me here so that we can study together."

That's exactly what we did. It wasn't always easy, but we worked at it. And I know Sarah was happy with the *A* she got on the next history test.

I let that pass. We opened our books and started to read over the chapter.

"Look at the part where it talks about prejudice," I said. I waited. Sarah wasn't moving. "Come on," I said.

Then I looked at her. She had tears in her eyes. "What's wrong?" I asked.

"I can't find it," she said. "I can't read as fast as you can." She turned away.

Suddenly, I understood why Sarah hadn't wanted to work with me. "It's okay," I said.

8

It sounded good so far. But what he said next didn't!

"I'll be assigning 'study buddies.' Together you'll read over the material in this chapter. Then you'll come up with your own ideas about *prejudice*—and ways of fighting it."

He called out the names of the people who would be working together. My heart sank when I heard my name. "Rosie Acosta, you'll work with Sarah Jonsen."

Sarah Jonsen! The girl on the soccer team who had laughed at me! I couldn't believe it! When I looked at her, she didn't look very happy. Well, neither was I.

All that week, I tried to avoid Sarah. I didn't say anything to her about our working together. She didn't say anything to me. Of course, it was impossible not to see her on Thursday at soccer practice.

A few of the kids tried to show me some of the plays. But I didn't pass the ball quickly enough. The others always got to it before I could pass. Then it wasn't long before Sarah had the ball and was racing down the field with it.

6

The next afternoon, I headed for the library to study. I had just opened my books when I felt someone looking over my shoulder. It was Sarah.

"What are you doing here?" I blurted out.

"Trying to find you," she said.

My heart sank. "I guess we should start our history project," I said.

"I guess so," said Sarah. But she didn't sound as if she meant it. I felt myself getting pretty hostile.

"Well," I said, "I don't care if you don't want to work with me. I'm not going to let it ruin my history project."

Sarah laughed. "You don't have to worry about that," she said. "You're a brain, aren't you?"

7

Welcome to the Rain Forest

by Susan McCloskey

HARCOURT BRACE & COMPANY

From the Library
of

_____

A Short Guide
to the Rain Forest

bromeliads [brō•mē′ lē•ad′] These rain forest plants have stiff leaves and roots that get water from the air.

curare [kyōo•rär′ re] Some people in South American rain forests use the curare plant to make poison arrows.

fungus [fung′əs] Fungi are plants that have no leaves, flowers, or green color. Mushrooms are one kind of fungus.

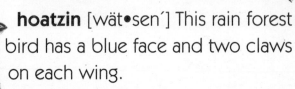

hoatzin [wät•sen′] This rain forest bird has a blue face and two claws on each wing.

shaman [shä′ mən] A shaman is a person who can cure people of many diseases.

tapir [ta′ pər] This animal looks like a pig with a hippo's ears.

People all over the world are trying to save the rain forest. I hope they succeed, because it is my home and I love it.

Thanks for visiting me!

Welcome to the rain forest! It has been home to my family for many, many years. It is my home, too. I'm glad you've come for a visit. Come on! I'll show you around.

My home is full of wondrous plants and animals. See how that vine twists its way up to the sky.

And look at the bromeliad plant! It is a strange one. There is a tiny pond in its center. It's filled with rain water!

Some snails and beetles spend their whole lives in this pond. Salamanders lay their eggs in it. Tree frog babies grow up there.

You may already know that the rain forest is disappearing. People are cutting it down and burning it to make way for crops and for cattle.

Even from my village we can see smoke from the smoldering ashes of the forest. And once a rain forest is gone, a new one never emerges.

Scientists are hurrying to study the rain forest before it is too late. They are afraid that medicines they don't know about will be destroyed. What a shame that would be!

Something else that comes from these vines is curare. Some people of the rain forest dip their arrows in the curare when they hunt. An animal struck by such an arrow cannot move.

The visiting scientist told me that doctors use curare, too. They sometimes give it to someone before a heart operation. It helps relax the heart muscles.

Did you notice that this plant grows on a tree instead of on the ground? That way, it is high above the forest floor. There, enough light and rain can reach it.

See what a bright flower the plant has. This is so that insects will see it and come to get its pollen.

There are thousands of insects in the rain forest. Here is one of them. It is a leaf-cutter ant.

These ants use their strong jaws to cut off pieces of leaves. They carry the pieces back to their nests underground. There they chew the pieces into mush. A fungus can grow on this mush. The fungus is the leaf-cutter ants' food.

chemicals that taste bad to the insects. It turns out that some of these chemicals also cure diseases.

My people also use plants to help them get food.

These boys are fishing. They shake pieces of vines into the river. The pieces contain a fish poison. Fish that get near it die.

Soon dead fish will rise to the top of the water. Then the boys will gather the fish and take them home.

The scientist was full of questions.

"What plants do you use? How do they work?"

That scientist found out that he could learn a lot from the shaman. Now he has come back to my village to work with him.

The rain forest has more plants with medicines in them than other places in the world. I asked the scientist why.

He said that it was probably because of all the insects. Insects can harm plants. So the plants make

The river is a road that winds through the rain forest. Let's follow it until we get to my village. Watch carefully! The river road is full of surprises.

Look. That bird is a hoatzin. See how it uses the claws on the ends of its wings to help it climb? Scientists say that this is one of the world's oldest birds. Some hoatzins just like this one may have been alive 50 million years ago!

The animal at the water's edge is a tapir. It is very shy.

This is my village. It's very small, and few people come here to visit. But last year a scientist came. He wanted to study our plants. This is because many rain forest plants contain medicines. They can cure diseases.

People here have used plant medicines for many, many generations. My grandmother knows a lot about such medicines.

Once when I was little, I had a toothache. My grandmother made tea from the bark of a tree. I drank the tea and the pain stopped. My grandmother knows how to cure stomach pains, headaches, and many other things.

There is someone who knows even more about plants than my grandmother. It is the shaman. A shaman is a very wise person who knows how to heal.

Last year, a man from another village brought his young son here. The boy was very sick. The shaman crushed some plants. He made a tea and told the boy to drink it. Very soon the boy was much better.

The visiting scientist watched the shaman cure the boy.

Lizard and the
Big Noisy

by Andrew Willett

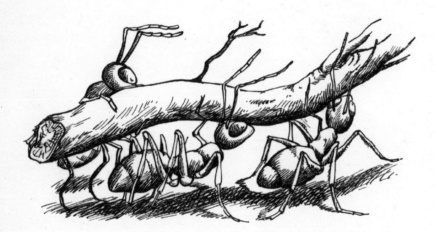

HARCOURT BRACE & COMPANY

From the

library of

The ants had done their job well. I thanked them as they left.

The Big Noisy did not come back. Then the cactus plants were content. They began to tell their stories again. Now every night I lie safe on my rock and listen to them.

They sometimes tell a new story. They tell about Lizard, whose clever plan saved his friends.

The sun still shines. The coyotes still laugh. Life is pretty good.

I am a lizard and my life is pretty good. The sun shines. I eat bugs. The cactus plants tell me stories.

My home is under this rock. Cactus plants are all around me. When the day starts, the first thing I see is the sun, rising behind them. The sunlight washes over them and their needles look like fire. It's a beautiful sight.

Soon the sun is a little higher and the air is warm. I go looking for bugs to eat. Out here in the scrubland there are plenty of flies and beetles and other insects. If it has lots of legs, it's for me.

I spend my time wandering over rocks and under plants. I look in holes and around corners. I jump out at crickets and spiders and I eat them.

There's not much more to tell you about my day, really. I eat. I rest. I sleep in the sun.

When the sun starts to set, I can hear the coyotes laugh. I never know what they're laughing at, and I don't ask them. Coyotes are very strange.

But when I hear them, I know it's time to head home.

Sure enough, the Big Noisy came in the night. I heard its roar. I smelled its hot, smoky breath. I saw the horrible fire of its eyes.

I heard voices. Heavy footsteps stopped as they reached the mesquite. Then we sprang our trap.

Thousands of fire ants charged. They rushed out from under the mesquite branches. They flowed like a river toward the Big Noisy. The men howled when they saw the ants! The heavy footsteps turned and quickly left.

The Big Noisy roared away. I ran to the top of a cactus and watched it go.

The sun was setting when I brought the last beetle to my rock. The ants were there. And what a job they had done!

The red light of the sunset shone on something new. The ants had built big piles of old mesquite branches around the cactus grove. They had dragged the dry, thorny branches from all over and piled them high.

I thanked the ants for their help. Some of them left, carrying the beetles and singing. The others took their places.

I went to my rock and waited for the Big Noisy to come back.

By nightfall I am back on my rock. I sit here until the stars come out and the cactus plants start to talk.

Only the oldest ones tell stories. The young ones just look up and listen.

The cactus plants tell stories about the beginning of the world. They tell "How Scorpion Made the Moon" and "How Woodpecker Met Cactus." They tell stories about Ring-Tailed Cat. They tell stories until long after I'm asleep.

As I said, life is good. But one night, not long ago, something happened that almost ruined everything.

I was nearly asleep. A very old cactus was telling a story about Ring-Tailed Cat that I had heard before. And then the Big Noisy came.

The Big Noisy had eyes brighter than the moon and a wide square face. It growled up to the edge of the cactus grove and it stayed there. Its hot breath smelled like metal and smoke.

What did it want? It did not speak. It only growled. I heard people's voices. There was a tearing, crashing sound. And then the Big Noisy left.

The cactus plants were silent. I asked them to explain what had happened, but none of them would talk to me. In the morning I saw for myself. The Big Noisy had taken one of them away.

4

The ants went off to get to work on my plan. I went looking for beetles.

Thirty beetles is a lot of beetles. So many beetles could feed all the fire ants for days. But I knew that the ants were my best hope. I knew that they would make my plan work.

So I hunted. When a lizard stalks in the desert, hunting for bugs, it looks everywhere. I hunted across rocks and under plants. I hunted in holes and around corners.

And by the end of the day, I had all the beetles I needed.

9

I didn't sleep a wink all night. The sun rose. Morning came.

Suddenly, I had an idea. I knew how to stop the Big Noisy! But I needed help. I scurried down from my rock and kept running until I found the fire ants. They were on patrol, looking for food.

"Ants! I know a way to save the cactus plants, but I will need your help. Will you come?"

I told them my plan. But they just shook their heads. They couldn't, they said. Everyone in their nest was counting on them to bring home food.

Well, if there is one thing I am good at, it is catching bugs. I offered to find thirty beetles for them if they would come and help. We had a deal.

8

Early that same morning some coyotes came. They wanted to see the hole where the cactus had been.

"What happened?" I asked the coyotes. "Where did the cactus go? Why won't the rest of them talk?"

The biggest coyote looked at me.

"They are silent because they are sad," he said. "The Big Noisy comes with people from the city. The people want cactus to plant outside their homes. Now that the Big Noisy knows where to find the cactus, it will keep coming back.

"You and your rock may be alone out here soon, lizard."

5

"But that's not right!" I shouted. "The cactus plants belong here! Together! Not scattered, far away! Who will tell the stories?"

"If you want to hear them tell stories, you'll have to go visit them." The coyote laughed. "If you can find them.

"Lizard, people are stronger than animals. They change our habitat all the time. We have to adapt.

"If you like stories, you'll have to find new ways to hear them."

I was very angry.

"I will not adapt! The people can't do this! I'll find a way to stop them! I'll stop them all by myself, if I have to!"

The coyotes ran into the hills, laughing.

All day I waited for the Big Noisy to return.

At midday when the sun was high above my head, I was angry. At sunset when the shadows were long on the ground, I was angrier.

The stars came out. I felt like thunder and lightning. I felt like fire.

After a while the Big Noisy came.

"GO AWAY!" I screamed. "LEAVE THE CACTUS PLANTS ALONE!" I thrashed my tail on the rock. I showed my claws. "THEY DON'T BELONG TO YOU!"

But the Big Noisy wasn't listening. I heard voices. I heard them pull another cactus out of the ground. Then the Big Noisy left.

TAKE-HOME BOOK

How Frog Lost His Tail

retold by Deborah Eaton

HARCOURT BRACE & COMPANY

From the

library of

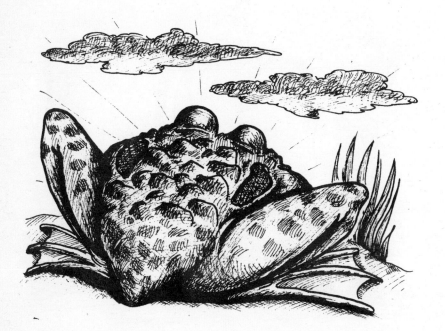

That is why, even today, every frog starts out as a tadpole with a big wavy tail. But that nice new tail disappears as the frog grows.

And that is why, if you listen, you can hear Frog out there on warm nights. He's still complaining.

"Grrump, grrump, grrump."

What a lump!

You know who I'm talking about. Frog, that's who. He's the one with the body like a blob of mud.

This story is about him. It happened *way back when* in Africa.

Old Frog knew he was ugly. How could he forget? All the other animals teased him and called him names.

Frog didn't like it one bit. But what could he do? There was no getting around it. He *did* resemble a lumpy, green rock.

Frog was tired of all the teasing. He didn't want to hear it. He tried stopping up his ears with mud. But that didn't work. He couldn't hear his dinner buzzing.

He tried disguising himself as things in his surroundings. First, he tried to look like a rock in a river. But that didn't work either. A river rock doesn't have a long, sticky tongue. Every time Frog tried to catch a fly, he gave himself away.

Then the animals just teased him harder.

In half a blink of an eye, Animal Father took away Frog's new tail.

"You did not do a good job here," he said to Frog. "You were mean and unforgiving. From this time on, no frog will ever forget what you did."

One dry and dusty day, someone new came to the waterhole.

Frog was having fun, splashing mud up onto Bush Buck's face. He heard a deep voice say, "Mmm, Mmm! I think I'll have a nice, cool drink of water."

Frog didn't even look up.

"Go away!" he croaked. "There's not enough water here for you! I'm the keeper of the waterhole and what I say goes."

"Oh, REALLY?"

It was a very deep voice. It was a voice like a deep-down cave. Uh-oh. It was Animal Father. Frog sank down in the mud until all you could see were his google eyes. But it didn't do him a lick of good.

Are you feeling sorry for Frog? Well, don't be too quick to judge. Frog wasn't just lumpy. He was grumpy, too.

All night long, Frog sat in the dark, grumbling. "Grrump, grrump, grrump."

All day long, Frog sulked in the mud, thinking. He was not thinking nice thoughts. Oh, no! He was thinking of ways to get back at the other animals. He wanted to make them sorry.

Once in a while, Frog would get a sly smile on his lumpy face. I won't even *tell* you what he was thinking then. You don't even want to *know*!

But he was one mad lily-pad-hopper!

One day, Frog was thinking his thoughts when a wart-hog came by.

"Hello, Bug Breath," Wart-hog said.

Frog didn't even look at him.

"Jelly Belly!" said Wart-hog. "Grump!"

That did it.

"Don't you dare mimic me!" roared Frog. "Why, you're as ugly as muck yourself!"

Nobody talked to Wart-hog like that.

"I may look a little rough," he growled. "But at least I have these handsome, white tusks. They're as sharp as sharp can be." Wart-hog lowered his head. "*If you get my meaning.*"

Frog did. He ducked under the water and hid.

4

A noticeable change came over Frog when he got his big new job at the waterhole. He got worse!

It was a very dry year. All the other waterholes were empty. Frog liked that. It gave him more chances to be mean!

Not one animal drank in peace. Frog only let them take little sips. Sometimes he splashed water in their faces. He played all sorts of silly tricks, too. He would jump out of the water and yell "BOO!" just as Lion was taking a big swallow. Mostly, though, he yelled and nagged.

"You're not drinking fast enough," he yelled at Hyena. "Go away!"

"You're messing up all the good mud," he nagged at Wart-hog. "Get out of here!"

I tell you— that frog was green and mean!

9

When the other animals saw what Animal Father had done, they felt bad. They remembered all the mean names they had called Frog.

One by one, the animals came by to say they were sorry.

"We didn't mean it," said Bush Buck.

"You've got yourself one fine tail, there," purred Lion.

"No hard feelings," growled Wart-hog.

But do you know what? Nothing they said made a pinch of difference to Frog. He was still mad.

8

Now, when even a wart-hog makes fun of your looks, you know it is time to do something.

Old Frog made up his mind. And the very next morning, he hip-hopped over to see Animal Father.

"Father!" Frog cried. "You've got to help me. I'm sick of being ugly."

"Ugly?" said Animal Father. He had a voice like a deep-down cave. "A frog is a frog. You look fine."

"No, no!" Frog hopped up and down. "Bush Buck has those big, brown eyes. Lion has that golden mane. Even Wart-hog has those handsome, white tusks. It isn't fair! What about me?"

5

Animal Father thought for a long time. He liked to be fair about these things.

"All right, Frog," he said at last. "You may have a point. How about this? I could give you a tail." He scratched his chin. "I have a special technique that should work."

"My very own tail?" shouted Frog. "Do it! Do it!"

"Hey! Slow down, there!" Animal Father's voice rumbled like thunder. "If I give you a tail, then you must do something for me. You must be keeper of my waterhole.

"My waterhole is always full. It enables all my children to drink during the dry years. It is important to their survival." Animal Father pointed a big finger. "You must keep it clean and watch over it. And you must welcome all the other animals to it."

"I'd be great at that!" Frog said. And he smiled his sly smile.

So old Froggy got himself a tail!

Believe me, that mud-thumper was one excited frog. Oh, my! How he admired himself! He thought he was so pretty!

You should have seen him, prancing around on those big green feet, waving that tail like a flag. It was a sight!

6

7

TAKE-HOME BOOK

Sonora

HARCOURT BRACE & COMPANY

by Steven Otfinoski

From the Library of

Desert Facts

- Desert animals get water in unusual ways. The kangaroo rat can get enough water out of the seeds it eats. Some large animals get water from the meat they eat. The desert cockroach can actually draw water out of the air! One kind of worm, the nematoda, completely dries up in the desert heat, but remains alive. When it rains, the worm fills up with water and wiggles again!

- The giant saguaro cactus can grow to be 50 feet tall and can live for 150 to 200 years. A saguaro can hold up to 6 tons of water in its trunk. If you need water in a desert, a cactus is where to find it. (It will be hot, bitter, and a little slimy!)

- Roadrunners, just 9 inches tall, can run 20 miles per hour.

13

The cool rain brings out bigger hunters, too, like coyotes and a mountain lion. They will hunt and eat before the morning comes.

Then the desert day will start all over again.

This is life in the Sonora Desert. It is a place of strange beauty. Here many plants and animals make the most of their harsh homeland.

It is the beginning of a new day in the Sonora Desert in Arizona. The sun rises over the dry, flat land. Some animals are waking up.

Tiny birds who reside in the saguaro cactus sing sweetly. Their homes are sculpted out of the giant cactus.

Other animals are going to bed. Bats and owls have been up all night hunting. They fly into caves and trees. They will sleep there all day.

The sun rises higher in the sky. The desert grows hotter. A long, green lizard glides onto a rock. There it basks in the sun's heat.

Other animals come out, too. A peccary chews on a prickly pear cactus. The peccary is a kind of hairy pig with tusks. It eats the cactus to get the water inside it. Water is hard to find in the desert.

The desert cools off quickly as night comes. Now the hunters come out to look for food.

A pack rat comes out of its hole to find some plants to eat. But another hunter sees it.

An owl swoops down and grabs the rat in its claws. It takes it back to its nest to eat.

The rain ends as suddenly as it began. The sun shines once again, but only for a short time.

Night is coming. As the sun sets, the sky fills with deep purples and bright pinks. It is a beautiful sight.

Many animals don't like the burning heat. They spend the day in underground holes and tunnels. It's much cooler down there.

Kangaroo rats dig a whole network of tunnels for themselves. These rodents have short front legs and big, strong hind legs, like a kangaroo.

It is noon now. The sun beats down on the desert and its creatures. It is very hot. The birds have stopped singing. Everything is still.

The peccary is resting in the shade of a saguaro cactus. The cactus stands tall, like a sentinel in the desert sand.

Even the lizard can't take the sizzling heat. It crawls between two large rocks. It's cooler there.

Plants need the rain, too. The barrel cactus soaks up rain into its trunk. The trunk swells to an enormous size. The cactus will slowly shrink again as it uses up the water.

TAKE-HOME BOOK

Bear Pie

by Anne W. Phillips

HARCOURT BRACE & COMPANY

Harcourt Brace School Publishers

From the Library of

____

"A frontier family can't let a little thing like that stop them," said Ma. "And this frontier family aims to succeed."

Ma set the pie plate on the table. She had sprinkled the crust with some of their precious sugar.

Then she had poked a picture in the crust and baked it.

Becky looked at the picture and started to laugh. There was a bear with a pail on its nose.

"If we can't have berry pie, we'll have bear pie," Ma said with a grin. "For a brave girl's birthday."

Becky grinned, too. She looked around the table at her family.

"A real frontier birthday," she said.

12

Becky swung the shiny tin pail. She skipped down the path to the creek.

Today was her tenth birthday. It would be her very first birthday on their new land.

There wouldn't be presents and a party, as she used to have back home. But Ma had promised to bake a birthday pie. All Becky and Sammy had to do was pick the blackberries.

1

Pa had read about the land in a newspaper back east. "Lots of opportunities out west," he had said. "We'll be a frontier family."

They had sold almost everything. Then they packed the rest in a wagon and headed west.

Ma sighed when she saw the little cabin made of logs. Then she rolled up her sleeves with a look of determination. She unpacked the dishes from the barrels of straw. She shook out her quilts. She swept the dirt floor.

Now even Ma said the cabin felt like home. "A settler home," she said.

Becky wasn't so sure. She missed her best friend, Millie. And she didn't like sharing a bed with her big sister Rachel.

It was worse for Sammy, though. Sammy had to share with their big brother Josh, and Josh snored.

Sammy told the story of the bear again at supper.

"That's my brave girl," said Pa. He smiled at Becky.

Josh promised to look for the pail the first chance he got.

Rachel promised to bake Becky a pie when the blueberries got ripe. "If the bear doesn't get them first," she said.

"Pie!" cried Ma. "I almost forgot."

She went to the cupboard and took out a pie plate.

"But, Ma," said Becky, "we lost all the berries. I threw them at the bear."

Under the sand, a spadefoot toad is awakened by the sound of falling raindrops. It digs itself out of the sand. It gobbles up insects that have come out in the rain.

The toad lays its eggs in the puddles that form. Its young need the water to grow into tadpoles. And the tadpoles need time to change into toads before the puddles dry up. Not a moment must be lost.

When its work is done, the spadefoot toad will go back to its home under the ground. There it may stay as long as nine months before coming out again.

A kangaroo rat has left its tunnel to take a look around. But it moves quickly. The ground is covered with a mantle of burning hot sand.

The kangaroo rat scurries along on its hind legs. Its tiny feet barely touch the desert sand. It sees a small, dark hole and runs for it.

8

5

The kangaroo rat has made a mistake. This hole is the home of a tarantula spider. The spider crouches inside the hole, feeling the vibrations in the sand as the kangaroo rat comes closer.

The kangaroo rat swerves at the last minute. Perhaps it smells the tarantula or perhaps it is just avoiding the unknown. It turns and scampers back to its own safe tunnel.

The tarantula doesn't run after the kangaroo rat. It's too hot for that. It goes back down into its underground home. The kangaroo rat is lucky this time. It won't be eaten.

The weather changes fast in the desert. It is now late afternoon. Dark clouds appear with little warning. They cover the sun. A bolt of lightning flashes across the sky.

The peccary runs for cover under a bush. Fat raindrops splash against the dry, sandy ground.

This is the first rain in the desert for many weeks. It is like the beginning of a new era.

Becky was thankful, too.

She could not help thinking about the lost pail, though. The lost berries bothered her, too. There would be no birthday pie today.

For the rest of the afternoon, Becky helped feed the chickens. She helped weed the garden, too. There was always work to be done, even on a birthday.

10

"Wait up, Becky!" Sammy called.

Becky slowed down to let her little brother catch up.

"Are we almost there?" he asked.

"Almost," said Becky. "The berries are right down by the creek."

And there they were, just around a bend in the trail. Prickly bushes with big black berries were just waiting to be picked.

3

Becky and Sammy set to work filling the bucket.

"One for the bucket. One for me," sang Sammy.

Soon their lips were purple with berry juice. Their arms were covered with scratches.

Becky put a last handful in the bucket. Enough for a pie and then some, she thought.

"Let's go, Sammy," she said.

Sammy didn't answer.

Becky turned to look for him.

She froze.

"Well?" Ma asked.

"The bear has the pail," said Becky.

"Bear!" cried Ma. "What bear?"

"The one that almost got me," said Sammy.

Becky let Sammy tell the story. When he had finished, Ma pulled them both close.

"That was quick thinking, Becky," Ma said. "I will look for the pail later. I'm just thankful you are both all right."

They burst into the cabin and slammed the door. Ma was rolling out pie crust.

"Where are the berries?" she asked. "And where is the pail?"

The tin pail! Becky had forgotten all about it. Ma had traded with Peddler Joe for that pail just a few days before. Peddler Joe came every few months to supply the settlers with things they couldn't make.

There stood Sammy, not far away.

And there stood a bear, swiping at the berry bushes with a huge brown paw.

"Sammy," whispered Becky, "back up very slowly."

Sammy didn't move.

"Sammy! Back up over here by me."

This time Sammy heard. Cautiously, he took a step backward.

The bear turned its big head and stared straight at him.

Becky's heart thumped so hard she was sure the bear could hear.

What could they do? Bears could be dangerous. Pa had warned them. Should she run back and get Pa? Should they climb a tree? Could bears climb trees? She didn't want to find out.

The bear took a step toward Sammy.

Becky didn't stop to think. She threw the pail of berries right at the bear's nose. The pail bounced off and rolled along the ground. Berries scattered everywhere.

The bear shook its head. Then it sniffed at the berries. It began to gobble them up.

Becky grabbed Sammy's hand. Slowly they took one step backward. Then another. The bear was pawing inside the pail for the last of their berries.

As soon as they rounded the bend in the trail, Becky ran, dragging Sammy with her. They raced all the way back to the cabin.

Harcourt Brace School Publishers

TAKE-HOME BOOK

The New Teacher

by *Steven Otfinoski*

HARCOURT BRACE & COMPANY

From the

library of

Mrs. Juarez looked at her students' faces.

"I guess you like Ms. Clemens a lot," she said.

"She turned out to be okay," said Cooper.

"Well, you'll see her again, soon," said Mrs. Juarez. "You see, you're not the only ones who like Ms. Clemens. She's coming back, as soon as she's better. She's going to be teaching fifth grade, full time, from now on."

Cooper grinned. It looked as if the new teacher was fitting in just fine after all.

It was the first day of school after the Thanksgiving holiday. Cooper walked into Mrs. Juarez's fourth grade room and took his seat. But something was wrong. Mrs. Juarez wasn't there.

A woman sat at Mrs. Juarez's desk. She was younger than Mrs. Juarez. She was wearing a suit.

"Hello, class," she said. "I'm your new teacher. I just moved to the city from a little town about a hundred miles from here. My name is Ms. Clemens."

"Where's Mrs. Juarez?" Cooper asked the new teacher.

"Mrs. Juarez had to go to Texas," explained Ms. Clemens. "Her mother is ill."

"Will she be back soon?" asked Karen Reed.

"I'm sure she won't be gone for long," Ms. Clemens assured her. "But I'll be your teacher until she returns."

Cooper couldn't believe it. They all loved Mrs. Juarez. She was the best teacher in the school. Now she was gone.

Everybody missed Mrs. Juarez. It was hard to get used to someone new.

Cooper and the other kids were in for another surprise when they came to school on Monday. Standing in front of the room was Mrs. Juarez!

Everyone was happy to see her.

"Why didn't anyone tell us you were coming back?" asked Stan.

"Well, I wasn't going to come back until Wednesday," explained Mrs. Juarez. "But then the principal called me. He said Ms. Clemens had hurt her ankle. So I came back two days early."

"Quick!" cried Cooper. "Hold up the banner!" The kids lifted a big, bright banner and held it high.

Ms. Clemens looked up and saw it. She gave a crooked smile and started running a little better. The students cheered as she crossed the finish line.

"We thought you were giving up!" cried Stan.

"I was," said Ms. Clemens. "I twisted my ankle and it really hurts. But when I saw your banner, I knew I had to finish. Thank you for cheering me on!"

A doctor came to look at her foot.

"You'd better get home and rest it," he said.

Ms. Clemens seemed nervous all the time. When she got impatient, her voice cracked.

One day, during a writing lesson, Stan told Ms. Clemens that they usually started by telling stories to warm up.

"If that's Mrs. Juarez's custom, let's try it," Ms. Clemens said. Then she told a story that was supposed to be funny. But everyone felt indifferent about it. No one laughed. Ms. Clemens blushed.

Cooper was beginning to feel a little sorry for Ms. Clemens. She was like the new kid in school. And like a new kid, she was having trouble fitting in. But this new kid was the teacher.

One evening, Cooper was taking out the trash out when a jogger waved at him. It was Ms. Clemens! Her purple sweat suit had a miniature alligator on the front.

"Cooper!" said Ms. Clemens. "I wish you could see the expression on your face! Teachers jog too, you know." She wasn't shy, the way she was at school.

"Hi, Ms. Clemens," Cooper called out. "Don't stop because of me," he answered.

"Oh, I've done my five miles."

"You ran five miles?" Cooper asked in surprise.

"I run five miles every day," she answered. "I'm training for the race in the park next month."

4

The big race was held on a Saturday. Crowds of people cheered for the runners.

Cooper and some other kids from Ms. Clemens' class were waiting at the finish line.

The first runners pounded past.

Then Karen cried out, "There she is!"

Finally they saw Ms. Clemens running.

"Something's wrong," said Cooper.

It was true. Ms. Clemens' face was twisted with pain. She was limping. It looked as if she dreaded every step.

Cooper stayed after class.

"I hope you don't mind my telling the other kids about your running," he said.

"Not at all, Cooper," Ms. Clemens said. "In fact, I'm glad you did."

After that, Ms. Clemens seemed more comfortable. She smiled more often. Kids listened better to her in class. Some of them even stayed to talk with her after school.

8

Cooper had heard about that race. You had to be very good to run in it.

"You must be a real runner, then," he said.

Ms. Clemens smiled. It was a nice, big smile. He had never seen her smile that way in school.

"I like to run," she said.

"So does my dad," said Cooper. "But he never runs five miles!"

Ms. Clemens laughed. "Well, I'd better head home," she said. "My dog is waiting for his dinner."

She waved good-bye and ran on down the street. So she has a dog, too, Cooper thought.

5

The next day, Karen said, "Ms. Clemens said my scary stories don't appeal to her. I wish she'd get scared and run away!"

"That's funny," Cooper said. "She ran past my house just last night."

"What are you talking about?" Stan asked.

"She runs five miles a day," Cooper said. "She's going to run in that big race in the park next month."

"No way!" cried Karen.

"Ask her yourself," said Cooper.

"Is it true you run five miles every day, Ms. Clemens?" Karen asked in class.

Everybody looked surprised.

Ms. Clemens said, "Yes. Every day."

"Are you running in the big race?" asked Stan.

"I'm planning to," she answered.

Then the students asked a lot of questions about running. Ms. Clemens answered each question with a smile. It was the same big smile Cooper had seen the night before.

6

7

TAKE-HOME BOOK

The Golden Dream:
The Story of the
Transcontinental Railroad

by Barbara Reeves

HARCOURT BRACE & COMPANY

From the
Library
of

_____

Trains of Thought

The transcontinental railroad brought great changes to the United States.

- More immigrants from the East coast traveled by train to settle in the West.

- Thousands of new towns were built along the routes of the railroad.

- Railroads made it easier to ship goods across the country.

- People on trains shot at the huge buffalo herds. They almost wiped out the buffalo.

- Native Americans had had many uses for buffalo. When the great herds were gone, their way of life had to change.

A gold spike had been made to join the last two
rails. Leland Stanford and Thomas Durant were to
hammer the spike. Stanford had helped start the
Central Pacific Railroad. Durant was Vice President
of the Union Pacific. Both men swung with a silver
hammer. Both men missed!

As the crowd laughed, a Union Pacific engineer
took up the hammer. He drove in the gold spike.
Then the two train engines pulled forward and gently
tapped each other.

At last the golden dream had come true. The
East had met the West. A great nation was joined
together by the rails.

12

It is 1869. A silver hammer swings in the air.
Clang! The hammer crashes down upon a gold railroad spike. Clang! Again the hammer strikes. The
sound rings out like a bell as the spike drives into
the railroad bed.

A waiting crowd roars with excitement. A band
begins to play. The Union Pacific and Central Pacific
Railroads have been joined! For the first time, a railroad track stretches all the way across this land.

1

In the 1800s, transportation in the United States was growing and changing. Canal boats took people and goods from place to place in the East. Steamboats churned up and down the Mississippi River. Stagecoaches and wagons rolled along the dusty trails in the West.

Then came the railroads.

Trains were faster than boats or wagons. Trains were cheaper for moving goods. And trains could run any time of year, in any weather.

The railroads grew fast. In 1840, there were about 2,800 miles of track in the United States. By 1869, there were 30,000 miles of track.

Everyone wondered where the two railroads should meet. Finally, they agreed on a spot in Utah.

On May 10, 1869, two train engines were placed almost face-to-face. One was the Central Pacific's Jupiter. The other was the Union Pacific's Engine No. 119. Only a one-rail gap separated them.

Important people from the railroads gathered. Bands, speakers, and guests came, too. Then workers from both railroad companies joined together to put down the last rail.

Both the Central Pacific and the Union Pacific wanted to build as much track as possible. The more track they put down, the more money they would make. Each company rushed to outbuild the other.

The Central Pacific reached the Nevada border. Then it pushed toward Utah. The Union Pacific reached Utah, as well.

But there was still no railroad that carried people or goods from the Atlantic coast to the Pacific coast.

Meanwhile, the West was growing. Miners, prospecting for gold and silver, had rushed there. Farmers and ranchers were settling there. But the journey was very hard.

Some traveled by covered wagon. The trip was long, hard, and dangerous. It took many weeks.

Others traveled by ship. They sailed south. Then they got off the ship and crossed the jungles of Central America on foot. Then they got on another ship and sailed north again.

Still others traveled west by sailing around the tip of South America. There, the waters were stormy and dangerous.

People wanted a better way. Many were convinced that the answer was a railroad. It would have to go all the way across the continent of North America—a trans-continental railroad.

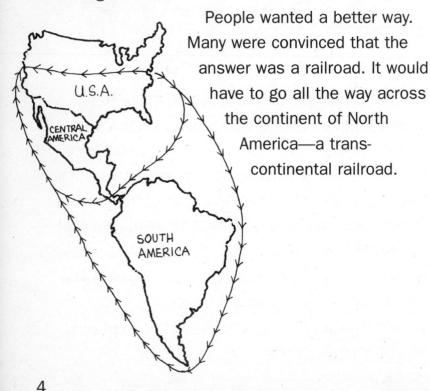

The workers on the Central Pacific faced a hard task from the start. The railroad had to go through the Sierra Nevada mountains. So, crews had to blast through high cliffs.

Workers were lowered in baskets down cliffs. They put explosives into the cliffs. Then they lit the fuses. Quickly, they were pulled up before the explosives went off.

Snow made the work dangerous, too. Thousands of workers died in the winter of 1866–1867. Many died blasting tunnels through the icy mountains. Others were killed by bitter cold or sudden snow slides.

Harcourt Brace School Publishers

Could these men handle the hard work of building a railroad? Many of the men weighed only about
120 pounds. They were often under five feet tall.

At first, Charlie Crocker's partners did not think
they could do it. Then Crocker reminded them of the
Great Wall of China. He said that if the Chinese
could build that huge wall, they could build a railroad.

He gave the Chinese workers a chance. They
were excellent railroad workers. They worked so well
that the railroad even sent to China to hire more
workers.

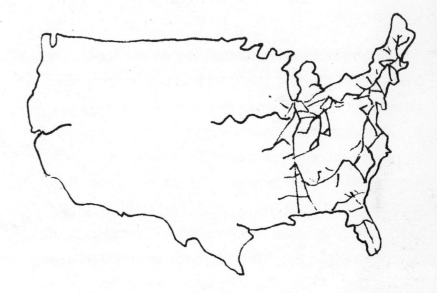

The government agreed. In 1862, Congress
passed a law to create this kind of railroad. They
offered land grants to companies who would build it.
Two companies were chosen. These were the Union
Pacific Railroad and the Central Pacific Railroad.

The Central Pacific began laying tracks east from
California. At the same time, the Union Pacific began
laying tracks west from Nebraska. This was where
track from the East already ended.

The dream of a transcontinental railroad was
beginning to come true.

The first step was to plan the route. Then work crews could prepare the road bed where the track would go.

The work crews had a very dangerous occupation. Their job was not easy. Some workers faced angry Native Americans who did not want the "fire road" on their land. Work crews had to blast through rocks and hills. Each rail weighed 500 pounds. Still, the crews often put down as much as three miles of track a day.

Those hard-working railroad men needed plenty of supplies to keep them going. So the railroad companies set up "work trains." These trains had kitchens, offices, stores, and sleeping areas.

The Union Pacific Railroad made its way west. The Central Pacific moved east.

The Union Pacific hired many workers from Europe. These people had come to America to claim citizenship. They were eager for work.

But so far, fewer people had settled in the West. The Central Pacific had trouble finding workers. What could the company do?

Charles Crocker, who supervised construction for the railroad, had an idea. During the California gold rush, many Chinese emigrants had left China to look for gold. They had settled in the West. Crocker decided to hire Chinese workers.

TAKE-HOME BOOK

HARCOURT BRACE & COMPANY

THE JADE PAINTBRUSH
A CHINESE TALE

retold by Eric Coates

From the
Library
of

"Give me some wind, so I can go see the fish," he said. Ma Liang painted the wind.

"More! More wind!" shouted the emperor. Ma Liang painted a huge storm cloud. Lightning danced all around. Winds rocked the emperor's boat.

"Enough!" cried the emperor in despair. "I will never get back to shore!"

And sure enough, that is what happened. The wind pushed the boat far, far across the sea. No one saw the emperor again.

And Ma Liang? He disappeared too. Maybe he went back to his village. Maybe he wandered from place to place, painting as he liked. No one knows. It is his secret.

12

Long ago, there was a boy named Ma Liang. Ma Liang loved to draw. Wherever he was during the day, he would find a stick. Then he would draw with it in the dirt. At night, the wind would whistle around the corners of his hut. Ma Liang would take cold charcoal from the fire. Then he would cover the walls with dragons.

Ma Liang dreamed of learning to paint. All he needed was a paintbrush. But brushes were costly. Ma Liang was too poor to buy one. In a big house nearby lived a famous artist. How Ma Liang wanted to watch as pictures appeared under the artist's hand!

1

One day, Ma Liang saw the artist sitting outside. The artist had a large sheet of paper spread across the ground. He was painting a mountain.

Ma Liang watched quietly for a long time. As he leaned closer, he noticed a whole jar full of brushes on the ground. If he had just one brush, he thought, he could paint anything.

In a shy voice Ma Liang asked, "Master, may I borrow a brush? I am too poor to buy one, and I want to be an artist."

The artist did not even look up.

"Why should I give you a brush?" he said gruffly. "A brush is a tool. It is not a toy. Go away and let me work!"

2

Won't you help me too?" He sighed. "I am a busy man," he said. "I get so tired. I would like to be able to look at the sea while I rest."

Ma Liang nodded. He painted the sea.

"Why don't you paint some fish?" asked the emperor.

"What kind of fish?" asked Ma Liang.

The emperor thought. "Golden fish," he said.

Ma Liang painted the golden fish, jumping up from the waves. Their gold fins sparkled.

11

The emperor could see that the paintbrush only worked for Ma Liang. He ordered his men to bring the boy before him.

Ma Liang had eaten nothing. His clothes were dirty and torn. Next to the guards he looked tired and helpless.

When the emperor saw him, he thought, "This boy is stubborn, but he is only a boy. He is nothing without his paintbrush. Look how poor he is! He cannot be very smart. I will trick him into doing what I want."

The emperor ordered food and a bath for Ma Liang. He had Ma Liang dressed in beautiful new silk clothes.

Ma Liang made a quick recovery. He was glad to be treated well. But he also remembered that the emperor could be very mean when he did not get his way.

Later, the emperor sent for Ma Liang again.

"I am sorry," the emperor said. "I was impatient. You have helped many people with your painting.

Ma Liang was stunned by what the artist said. But he was not discouraged.

He spent the rest of the day drawing. He drew leaves and branches all over the walls of his hut. When he lay down to sleep, it was like lying in a forest. He could almost see the trees move.

That night Ma Liang had a dream. In his dream, an old man with a white beard came to the door of his hut. He called Ma Liang's name. Then he held out a brush made of beautiful green jade.

"This is a special brush," he said. "Use it well."

When Ma Liang woke, the brush was still in his hand. He was amazed. Leaping up, he painted a bird. The bird jumped into the air and flew away. Next, he painted a peach. The peach turned ripe and fell into his hand. Ma Liang was delighted with his new brush. He went around his village and painted things people needed. He painted a pair of shoes. He painted herbs for making medicine. He painted food for people who were hungry.

Soon, everyone began to talk about Ma Liang. They talked about the wonderful things he did. More and more people came to ask for his help. It made Ma Liang feel good to help them.

4

Ma Liang arrived at the emperor's palace. He was pushed into a room full of paper. Then the emperor ordered him to paint a palace of gold.

Ma Liang shook his head "no."

The emperor became angry. His guards grabbed Ma Liang's arms and took him away. Then the emperor took away Ma Liang's paintbrush.

The emperor tried the paintbrush himself. He painted a palace of gold. But the gold bricks turned into plain rocks. Then the emperor painted a gold coin. But when he picked it up, it melted. The coin was made of butter.

9

Soon the whole village knew what had happened. Then the neighboring villages knew. Soon, men came to bring Ma Liang to the emperor.

The emperor had many palaces. Each was greater and more beautiful than the last. Still, he was not happy. He dreamed of building a palace of gold. But in all the empire, there was not enough gold to build such a palace.

Then he heard about Ma Liang. The emperor thought he had found the answer to his dreams.

"If the stories are true," he thought, "I can have as much gold as I want!"

8

One of the people who heard about Ma Liang was a merchant from a nearby town. The merchant was a greedy man. He thought of nothing but gold. Already he had more riches than anyone could need. This merchant sent for Ma Liang. He showed Ma Liang a long roll of paper.

"Paint gold coins!" he said. "I will reward you."

Ma Liang shook his head "no." The merchant ordered his servants to put Ma Liang in a barn. It was winter, and very cold.

"You will get no food until you paint those coins!" cried the merchant.

5

Late that night, the merchant went to the barn. Through a crack in the door, he saw Ma Liang. The boy was sitting next to a stove and making bread. In a rage, the merchant ran to get his servants.

When he returned with his servants, the stove was still burning. Ma Liang was nowhere to be seen. They ransacked the barn, turning over boxes and jars of grain. Then, in a corner, they saw a ladder.

The merchant climbed up the ladder. At the top was an open window. In the moonlight, he saw Ma Liang. The boy was running across a field. As the merchant watched, Ma Liang painted a horse and rode away.

6

Ma Liang rode for many days. Then he came to a village where no one knew him.

He knew he should not paint as he had. If he did, people would talk, and trouble would find him again. Now, when he painted, he always left something out. If he painted a fish, he left out some scales. If he painted a flower, he left out a petal. None of the pictures came to life. So, for a long time, Ma Liang lived peacefully.

One day he was painting in the village. A woman asked him to paint a crane. Carefully, Ma Liang painted. He left out the center of the crane's eye.

"That's very good," said a man who was watching. He patted Ma Liang on the back. Ma Liang's arm shook. A tiny drop of ink fell from the brush. It landed on the crane's eye.

The crane flapped into the air.

7

TAKE-HOME BOOK

The Night We Slept in the Barn

HARCOURT BRACE & COMPANY

by Kana Riley

From the

library of

Grandma opened her mouth, but Mike beat her. "When Grandma was a girl, she and her cousin Lilly . . ."

Danny cut in. "They slept in the hay . . ."

"Only it wasn't all wired up in bales then . . ."

"Whoa," laughed Dr. Stern. "That sounds like a great story. I'd like to hear all about it."

"Let's all have a picnic dinner in the hayloft. Then you can tell me the whole story."

Grandma smiled to herself. Maybe the old barn was starting a new cycle of its life.

Mike tugged on her sleeve. "Just don't get any ideas about rattling chains," he said.

"Grandma! There it is. The barn you and Lilly slept in." Mike pointed to the big red building.

Grandma smiled at Mike and his friend Danny. She pulled the car to the side of the road. "You still remember that story?" she asked.

Mike answered, "How could I forget?" Grandma always told that story, every time they visited the old farm.

Of course, Grandma didn't live here anymore. It wasn't even a farm. It was just an empty barn with an old house across the road.

Sometimes Mike wondered why his grandmother came here anymore. She must have loved the place a lot when she was a kid. But now it seemed to make her kind of sad.

Grandma would talk about how things used to be. She had lots of memories.

"The apple orchard was up on the hill. I remember the smell of the flowers and the sound of the bees. They'd come to collect nectar from the apple blossoms."

"The Kurowskys built their house where the orchard stood. A couple of trees are left. But I don't think they produce much of a yield anymore. My dad used to say nothing would nourish you like one of his apples."

The barn was her favorite place, though. "Look at it," she said. "It's just as straight and true as the day my grandfather built it. The silos have blown down. But the rest of it still looks just fine."

Before Grandma could get any more words out, the woman reached over to shake her hand.

"My name is Dr. Stern," she said. "Jane Stern. I just bought this house and barn. That's my office down there."

She nodded her head toward what used to be the store. then she said to Grandma, "You must be Earl Bartlett's granddaughter! Didn't he build this barn? A carpenter just said he'd never seen a barn of such good quality."

Grandma introduced the boys.

"You should be really proud to have a great-great-grandfather like Earl Bartlett," said Dr. Stern. "Now what was that about sleeping in the barn?"

Grandma turned to look down the road. "Do you see that yellow building? That used to be the general store. The next morning, we got up early. After we helped Grandpa milk the cows, he gave us each a nickel. We ran down to the store and bought candy."

Mike had not heard this part before. A nickel, he thought. That wouldn't buy much candy today.

Then the door of the old store opened. A young woman came out and walked up the hill.

"Hi," she called. "Do you like this old barn?"

Danny jumped off the wall and pointed to his grandmother. "She used to sleep in it!" he said.

Grandma started to explain. "You see, when I was a girl, my father . . ."

10

Mike liked to think about Grandma being a little girl on the farm. That's why he always asked her to tell about the night she slept in the barn.

"Cousin Lilly and I begged our parents all summer," she remembered.

"I remember you liked the hay," Mike said.

"Danny," said Grandma, "the top of that barn was filled with the sweetest-smelling hay. Piles and piles of it, all loose. Not all wired up in bales the way it is today.

"Lilly and I liked to jump in it, dig down in it and make nests. On rainy days we'd spend the whole afternoon playing there."

3

"What is the top floor of the barn called?" Mike asked.

"It's called the hayloft. Under that was the place where my father kept the farm machines—the hay mower and the mechanical tedder . . ."

"What's a tedder?" asked Mike.

"That's a machine that kicks up the hay after it's been cut. It helps the hay to dry."

That sounded like fun to Danny. "Did your father have a tractor?"

"He never did. He said the farm was too hilly. But I think he just liked horses better. He had two of them. Their names were Bessy and Stubby."

Grandma got out of the car. The boys hopped out after her.

"Well, you could almost see the hair rise up on those men's heads. They were so startled. They ran up the ladder to find out what had happened to us. Lilly and I just fell down in that hay and laughed."

"Was that the night your father decided to sleep in the barn too?" Danny asked.

"That's right. He stayed the rest of the night. I think even Cousin Lilly felt better with him there. She still says she was never afraid for a minute."

Mike shut his eyes. He pictured Danny and himself sleeping in the barn the way Grandma had.

Mike beat her to the punch line. "It was your grandpa, your father, and Uncle Cal," he said.

"That's right. They were rattling the chain on the tedder. They thought they could scare us. And they did!

"Then came the best part," Grandma chuckled. "The two of us just started screaming. You know, I don't think we even planned it. We didn't just make little *eeks* either. They were long, loud shrieks!

8

She pointed to the windows near the ground. "That's where the horse stalls were. They were on the ground floor. The cows were on the other side. My dad used to have about twenty-five of them."

The hay sounded pretty nice. But sleeping in the same building with horses and cows? Danny wasn't sure about that. "Did the cows and horses spend the night in the barn too?"

"They certainly did," Grandma said. She walked over and sat on the stone wall that ran beside the road. Grandma continued her story.

5

"Finally, when we were ten years old, our parents let us sleep in the hayloft one night. Lilly and I went down there after supper. We took our blankets and pillows." Grandma laughed at the memory.

"We talked and giggled for a long time. My cousin Lilly really liked to talk! It was very late when I saw it. Something that looked like a bird flew in front of that window."

"But birds sleep at night," said Mike.

"Yes," Grandma replied. "That's why I felt as if my heart would stop. I grabbed Lilly's and pointed.

"But my cousin Lilly was never scared of anything. She just laughed and threw hay on my head. It was only a bat, she said.

6

"Well, I tried to sleep. But I kept hearing noises. I knew that most of them were Bessy and Stubby shuffling in their stalls.

"Then I heard a sound that wasn't made by any animal. *Clink. Clink. Clink.*"

Mike knew the story well, but this part always scared him a little.

"Lilly heard the clink too. I think she tried to laugh, but I could tell that even she was scared. She grabbed me, and her hand was like ice.

"Lilly and I held hands and crept to the edge of the hayloft. We looked down. There in the shadows, we saw shapes that looked like bears."

7

TAKE-HOME BOOK

Alexander Graham Bell

by Deborah Eaton

HARCOURT BRACE & COMPANY

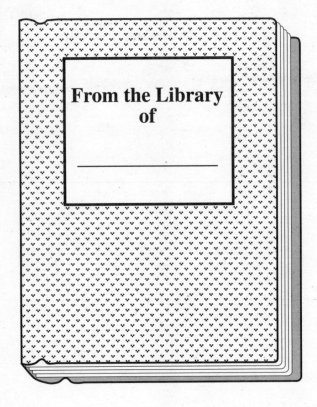

From the Library
of

_____

Phone Phacts

Today, Americans make over 800 million telephone calls per day!

The electric waves that carry our voices over telephone lines move 900,000 times faster than sound waves.

When Alexander Graham Bell first introdced the phone, people answered a call by saying "Ahoy! Ahoy!"

Watson made the first phone booth, when his landlady complained about the noise his phone made.

By 1915, our country was completely criss-crossed with telephone lines. Finally, even the East and West Coasts were connected. Alexander Graham Bell placed a call from New York to Tom Watson in California. People wondered what the famous inventor would say on this historic occasion.

Bell smiled and spoke into the telephone. "Watson! Come here," he said. "I want you."

On August 2, 1922, telephone service in the United States was shut down for one minute. All the telephone wires were silent for the first time since they had begun to buzz over forty years before.

On a windy hilltop near his summer home, Alexander Graham Bell, age 75, was being laid to rest.

On a winter day in 1847, a baby boy was born in Edinborough, Scotland. His mother held him close. She watched him kick his little legs. She touched his red face. But she couldn't hear him crying. The mother was almost completely deaf.

Her name was Eliza Bell. And the baby was her son, Alexander.

As little Aleck grew, he learned how to speak with his mother. He would put his mouth close to her forehead. Then he would speak very slowly and carefully.

Aleck's father and grandfather were both speech teachers. Aleck learned everything he could about how the voice makes sounds and how the ear hears. By the time he was 21, he was teaching speech, too. Like his mother, all of Aleck's students could not hear well.

There were always new inventions, too—lots of them.

"What a man my husband is!" Mabel exclaimed. "I am perfectly bewildered by the number and size of the ideas with which his head is crammed."

Bell still worked late at night. And he still hated noise or interruptions, even from phone calls!

Alexander Graham Bell was only 29 years old when he invented the telephone. He still had a long life to live. And that life had all the ingredients he needed for happiness.

There was Mabel, of course. They were married in 1877 and became the parents of two daughters.

And there was teaching. True to his word, Bell continued to teach all his life. He was a leader in teaching deaf people how to speak so that hearing people could understand. He started yet another school. He also became a lifelong friend of Helen Keller. Together, they helped the world see just how much people can accomplish.

Bell moved to Canada, then to Boston. His interest in education for the deaf continued. He taught speaking and lip-reading at a school for the deaf.

Later, he opened his own school. There he trained teachers to help deaf people speak.

At this time, there was a lot of discrimination against deaf people. Many deaf children were put into institutions. They weren't taught how to communicate. Bell felt this was terrible. He worked hard all his life to help deaf people connect with others. No matter how famous he got, he always listed his job this way: "teacher of the deaf."

When Bell was twenty-five, he met a nice young woman. Her name was Mabel Hubbard. Mabel, too, was deaf. Her father had hired Bell to help her learn to speak clearly.

Bell wanted to marry Mabel. But how could he? He was very poor. And there was another problem. Mabel's father was unhappy because Alexander was spending all his free time working on a foolish invention. It was called a telephone.

Bell's first love was teaching. But he had another love, too—inventing.

4

People say now that Bell's patent on the telephone—Patent Number 174,465—was the most valuable patent ever issued. But not everyone had the vision to see the telephone's usefulness right away.

Bell tried to sell his invention to Western Union Telegraph. They were not interested, they said, in an "electric toy."

So Bell gave demonstrations of his telephone. Soon people began to see just how useful a device it could be. Production began on telephones for businesses. Then many were installed in homes.

The first telephone service cost $20 per year. The first phone directory was printed in New Haven, Connecticut, in 1877. It listed eight names and numbers.

9

Bell and Watson managed to get the sound of a voice to carry over a wire. But it was weak and fuzzy. You couldn't understand the words. The two men tried many remedies to this problem. Nothing worked.

Then one March night, in 1876, they were trying a weaker electric current. Just as Watson was hooking up the wires, there was an accident. Bell had spilled acid on his clothes.

"Watson! Come here," he said. "I want you."

Watson came running. But the acid spill was forgotten. He had heard every word over the wire. The telephone worked!

When Alexander was a child, he invented a machine that took the husks off wheat. He and his brother also made a simple "speaking machine."

Bell was still inventing. He rented an extra room for $3 per week. He spent every night there, working.

A man named Tom Watson helped Bell. Watson knew a lot about electricity and engineering. He built the models they used to try out Bell's inventions.

Bell's first idea was to make a telegraph wire that would carry many messages at once. It would make communication a lot quicker. The telegraph idea was soon orphaned, however. Bell abandoned it when he had a new idea—a bigger idea.

What if we could send our voices along a wire? What if we could talk long-distance? People could stay in touch with friends and relatives. They could get help quickly from doctors and fire fighters. They could make business deals without messengers and letters.

Soon Bell was working furiously on his dream of a telephone. He spent every dime he had on equipment. And he spent every spare minute in his workroom.

People were worried about his health. They tried to get him to give up either teaching or inventing. But both jobs were too important to him.

Bell was a real night owl. He often worked on his inventions until three or four o'clock in the morning. He loved the silence of late night. He even stopped his clock so its ticking wouldn't bother him.

Poor Mabel must have spent a lot of time alone. And she worried about Alexander. She tried to get him to agree to stop working at midnight. It was no use.

Finally, she told him she was going to paint his portrait. In she walked one night with a big painting of an owl!

Alexander Bell laughed. Then he kept right on working.

TAKE-HOME BOOK

Century Club to the Rescue

by Molly Bridger

HARCOURT BRACE & COMPANY

From the
Library
of

_____

Then, as they were looking in the stream, a patch of water with a slick of swirling colors floated under the bridge.

"Uh oh!" Amanda said.

"Another problem to conquer," Sandy added.

Amanda and Sandy looked at each other.

"Century Club to the rescue!" they cried. And they ran off to tell the other members.

"Yuck!" Amanda exclaimed.

"What's the matter?" Sandy asked. Their class had walked halfway around the town's nature trail. Sandy was having a good time. This was better than being inside a classroom.

"Look at this mess!" Amanda said. She waved her hand at the litter on the side of the trail. "Look at the stream!"

As they crossed a wooden bridge, Sandy looked down at the water. Fishing line was tangled around the bushes. Soda cans poked up out of the mud. The stream's current tugged at a plastic bag caught between two rocks.

"At this rate, our descendants will have to wade through trash," Amanda said.

"Hey, we're only kids," Sandy said. "What can *we* do about it?"

"I don't know. Maybe we can have a class meeting. We would come up with some ideas," Amanda answered.

They spoke to Mr. Ortiz. He gave the class some time to talk about the problem. That's how the Century Club got started.

The kids in the club wanted to help their town stay beautiful for the next one hundred years.

2

Weeks after the movie was finished, Amanda and Sandy took another walk on the nature trail.

"There's almost no litter!" Sandy said.

"Not even in the stream," Amanda agreed. "It's beautiful."

"It's boring!" Sandy answered. "There's nothing else to do."

Amanda grinned at her friend. "But at first we were afraid that we wouldn't be able to really help. This is terrific!"

Sandy grinned back.

11

The members of the Century Club and their families met at school to watch their movie on television together. It was great!

In the days that followed, the club got hundreds of letters from people who thought their movie was wonderful, too. Many people asked to join the Century Club.

All the kids in the class had ideas to share.

"Members of the Century Club can go out each week and clean up the trail."

"Wouldn't it be better if people didn't drop litter in the first place?"

"Could we put up some signs?"

"Maybe we could have a meeting to tell people not to litter."

"Most people wouldn't come to a kids' meeting," Sandy said sadly.

"Then let's find another way to make them listen," said Amanda. "Maybe we could make a movie. That would get people to think more about the problem."

Everyone loved her idea.

Mr. Ortiz helped them plan. For a math lesson, they figured out how much it would cost to make a movie—and how they could earn the money. They did research and wrote a script.

"This is hard work," said Sandy.

"But it's fun," Amanda said.

"It will be when we make the movie," said Sandy.

4

One station called back a few days later.

"They said they'll show the movie tomorrow night, during the news," announced Mr. Ortiz.

Everyone in the Century Club was very, very excited.

9

The Century Club watched the movie together and were amazed. It was just three minutes long, but it said a lot.

"That's great!" Sandy said. "Now what?"

"Maybe a television station would be interested in your movie," Mr. Ortiz said.

"Let's write to all the stations," Amanda suggested.

So they did.

Amanda did a lot of reading.

"There are so many problems," she said. "Litter is just one little problem. The air is full of pollution. Chemicals are in our streams. We are going to need hours of movies to tell everyone everything."

"Let's take one step at a time," said Mr. Ortiz. "Today, litter. Tomorrow, the world."

"What if the world isn't listening?" Sandy asked.

"If only one person listens, it will be worthwhile," Mr. Ortiz replied.

Finally, they were ready to make the movie.

Some kids operated the camera. Others were in the movie.

They showed how a place looked before and after people littered.

They told how plastic bags and fishing line disrupted animals' lives. Sometimes, it even killed them.

Then they showed the eight huge bags of litter that the Century Club had picked up around the nature trail.

Amanda and Sandy spoke at the end.

"We started the Century Club so that our town will still be beautiful in one hundred years," Sandy said.

"We hope everyone in town will become members," Amanda added, "because litter is just one small problem. We want people who come after us to know we cared for the earth."

6

7

Harcourt Brace School Publishers

TAKE-HOME BOOK

HARCOURT BRACE & COMPANY

Listen to Your Mother

by Anne W. Phillips

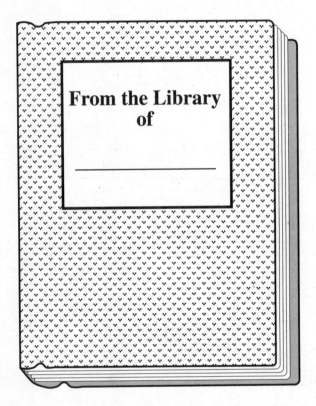

From the Library
of
_____

Helping Mother Earth

Make up a game to help save the earth.

In each square on this page, write something you can do to save the earth—or not save it! You can use the ideas in this book, or think of your own.

Now you need to make up the rules. What will you use for game pieces? How will you decide how far to move? What will happen if you land on a square that doesn't help to save the earth? How will someone win the game?

Now play the game with a friend!

13

So you'd better get busy. I want to see this planet sparkle.

Who says so?

Mother Earth, that's who.

And everyone knows you should listen to your mother.

Okay, everybody, listen up. This is your mother speaking. Your Mother Earth.

What's that you say? You didn't know I could talk?

It's true, I haven't said much for a millennium or two. But I've got a few things to say now.

You know how your mother always tells you to clean up your room? Well, I'm here to tell you to clean up the earth. Now, don't start waving your arms and yelling about oppression and kids' rights.

Just listen for a minute to what I have to say.

We've only got one planet. And we've got to take good care of it.

Let's start with the earth.

Yes, me.

I'm pretty important, you know. Without earth, where would you grow all your food? Where would you build your houses? Where would you put your feet?

Let's face it, you need me.

And so do all the plants and trees and animals that live on the earth with you.

Well, you see what I mean.

Pretty soon we'll have a chain reaction.

Pretty soon we'll have an earth that's safe and clean for all living things.

And that's something worth working for.

Let's not forget one of the most important things
of all on Earth.

You.

Yes, you.

Oh, I know, you're only one person. But if you
do just one thing to keep the earth clean and safe,

and another person does one thing,

and another person does one thing. . . .

So here are a few tips on how to take care of
the earth—for everybody's sake.

Don't litter.

Recycle paper, cans, and bottles.

Buy only things that you need. And find new
uses for old things instead of just throwing them out.

Use cloth napkins and rags instead of paper
napkins and towels.

Take your own shopping bags with you when
you go to the store.

Plant a garden.

There, that wasn't so hard, was it?

Now, what about the air?

You breathe it, in and out, over seventeen thousand times a day. Plants and animals breathe it, too.

Usually, you can't see the air. But lately I've been noticing a haze around some of the cities and factories. That's not just clouds, you know. That's pollution.

You can help save the plants and animals. Build a birdhouse or a nesting box. Put up a bird feeder. Plant fruit trees and berry bushes for the birds. Join a group that works to save endangered animals.

People aren't the only ones living on Mother Earth, you know.

Animals and plants live here, too. But some of them are endangered. That means there aren't too many of them left. Some plants and animals are extinct. That means none of them are left. No one will ever see them again.

We need to protect the plants and animals. They might be useful. Many of them are beautiful and interesting, too.

We share this planet together.

8

What can you do to help keep the air clean for all living things? There's a lot you can do.

Cars cause pollution, so ride a bike or walk when you can. You can use buses or subways. Or carpool with other people.

Pollution comes from power plants, too. If you use less electricity, there'll be less air pollution.

So turn off lights, televisions, and radios when you're not using them. Wear a sweater instead of turning up the heat.

Buy recycled paper. It takes a lot less energy to make paper from other paper than it does to make it from trees.

Plant a tree. Trees put fresh oxygen into the air for us to breathe.

See? There's plenty you can do.

A mother knows these things.

5

And don't forget water. Plants, people, and animals all need fresh water to live.

Seventy percent of the earth is covered with water. Almost all of that is salty sea water. Only about three per cent of the earth's water is fresh. Most of that is frozen in glaciers and ice caps.

That leaves about one percent of all the water on the earth for all of us to use.

That's not much, is it?

It's all we have, so let's take care of it.

How can you take care of water? There are plenty of ways. Many rivers and lakes in the United States are cleaner now than they were twenty years ago. People have worked to clean them up. Keep up the good work!

If you live near a stream or river, try to take care of it. You can help pick up litter on the river banks. You can watch for pollution in the water.

You can save water around the house. Turn off the faucet while you brush your teeth. Fill up the sink to wash dishes. Don't just let the water run.

If you've got a dripping faucet, help a grown—up fix it.

Take short showers—you'll still get clean!

TAKE-HOME BOOK

HARCOURT BRACE & COMPANY

Glouskabi and the Wind Eagle

retold by Jan M. Mike

From the

library of

About the Abenaki

The Abenaki (or Abnaki) lived west of the Penobscot River in what is now the state of Maine.

They gathered wild plants, nuts, berries, and roots. They hunted for deer, bear, moose, and wild ducks. They fished in rivers and lakes. They used nets for small fish and spears for larger ones. Clams, crabs, and lobsters rounded out their diet.

Glouskabi is a popular figure in Abenaki legends. The young Glouskabi is often a bit too adventurous for his own good. But he grows and learns. He becomes a wise and strong hero.

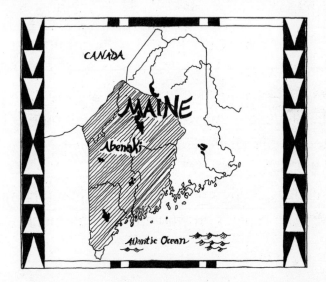

Two days later, Glouskabi finally returned to his home by the lake. Once more he paddled out onto the water to fish. A flock of ducks swam on the clear water. Glouskabi threw his net. A small breeze lifted it out over the silver fish.

Glouskabi smiled.

All his walking and climbing had made him quite hungry. But tonight he would eat a fine meal.

When Glouskabi was a boy, he lived with his grandmother in a small lodge by the lake. Glouskabi was tall, strong, and smart. But he didn't think things through. He often got into trouble.

One splendid day, when the wind was brisk and the sky was blue, Glouskabi decided to go fishing. He gathered his spears. He paddled his canoe out onto the bay. As he paddled, he composed a fishing song.

Glouskabi sang his song and lifted his net. But before he could throw the net into the water, a blast of wind blew his canoe back to the shore.

Glouskabi turned his canoe around. He paddled back out to the center of the lake. Once again, he lifted his net. But once again, the wind blew him back to shore.

Four times Glouskabi paddled out to the lake. Four times he lifted his net. And four times he was blown back to land.

Finally, he put his canoe away. Then he walked to the lodge he shared with his grandmother.

2

Glouskabi climbed down. He carried the wind eagle out. Then he carried him to the tallest mountain peak. He untied the eagle's wings.

Wuchowsen smoothed his feathers with his beak. Then he began to flap his wings.

Glouskabi smiled. He took a deep breath as a cool breeze stirred the air.

"Uncle," he said. "I know the wind must blow very hard sometimes. But I think the wind should blow softly sometimes, too."

"I see," Wuchowsen replied. "Well, I will think about what you say."

His grandmother sighed. "Grandson, the people need Wuchowsen and the wind. Wind keeps the water fresh and sweet. Wind brings the rain clouds. They water our food as it grows. Wind cools the air."

"Oh," said Glouskabi in an even smaller voice.

Glouskabi put his traveling moccasins back on. He walked through the hot forest. He passed delicate plants wilting. There was no breeze to cool them.

Finally, he reached the mountain. He was sweating and gasping for air. But he kept walking. He walked until he reached the hole where Wuchowsen lay.

"Uncle," Glouskabi called to the wind eagle, "what are you doing?"

"Nephew," Wuchowsen answered, "a bald boy promised to take me to a higher mountain. I let him tie my wings and carry me. But he dropped me here when he jumped over this hole."

"Well," Glouskabi said, "I will help you get out."

"Grandmother, where does the wind come from?" Glouskabi asked.

"Grandson, I don't think I want to answer your question," his grandmother replied. "Whenever you ask me such a question, you always get into trouble."

But Glouskabi could be a pest. He kept asking and asking. Finally, his grandmother could stand it no longer.

"Listen," she said, "and I will tell you. On top of a tall mountain, a great bird stands. He is Wuchowsen (Wū - chō - sen). He is the wind eagle. It is he who makes the wind blow."

Right then, Glouskabi decided to talk to the wind eagle. He put on his traveling moccasins. Then he tied a long rope around himself and walked into the wind.

All day, Glouskabi walked. The wind blew constantly. It blew the shirt right off his back.

Night fell. The wind blew even stronger. It blew the moccasins right off his feet.

At noon the next day, he began to climb the tall mountain. The wind blew his hair right off his head. Glouskabi closed his eyes and grabbed onto the rocks so he would not blow away. But still he didn't stop.

4

Feeling uneasy, Glouskabi went to his grandmother's lodge. As she nibbled an acorn cake, his grandmother stared at him.

"Glouskabi," she said. "You've made some trouble, haven't you?"

"Grandmother, it wasn't really my fault."

"Glouskabi, what have you done?" she asked.

Glouskabi told his grandmother all about his long journey. He told her about meeting the wind eagle. And then he told how he had tied up the eagle, and dropped it in the hole.

9

Glouskabi walked. He went down the mountain, across the valley, and through the forest. The monotony of each windless hour made him restless. He tried to fan his hand in front of his face. But that small, artificial breeze helped little.

In the morning, Glouskabi reached his home. He got his canoe and paddled onto the still waters of the lake.

Now the air was so hot that he could barely breathe. Mosquitoes buzzed. Gnats flew in a cloud around his head. The lake water no longer moved. A terrible smell filled the air.

8

On top of the mountain, a great bird flapped his huge wings. It was Wuchowsen, the distinguished wind eagle.

"Uncle," Glouskabi called out. "I have come to thank you for the strong winds that you blow."

"How kind of you." Wuchowsen flapped his wings faster.

Glouskabi shouted over the wind. "I think your wind would be even stronger if you stood on that mountain over there." He pointed to a taller mountain.

Wuchowsen's wings slowed, then stopped. He looked at the taller mountain.

5

"I cannot fly that high," said the wind eagle. "How could I get to that mountain?"

"I will help you," Glouskabi said. He untied the rope from around himself. "We can use my carrying strap to lift you up."

Wuchowsen lowered his head. He pulled in his wings. Quick as an otter, Glouskabi wrapped his rope around the bird. He tied the eagle's wings close to his body. The eagle could not move.

Then Glouskabi picked up Wuchowsen. Glouskabi walked toward the other mountain.

"Grandson, am I too heavy for you?" Wuchowsen asked. "If you untie me, I'll walk."

"You are light as a feather," Glouskabi panted. "Besides, we are almost there."

"But it looks very far away," said Wuchowsen.

"Oh, it is nearer than you think," gasped Glouskabi.

Between the mountains was a deep hole. As Glouskabi leaped across it, he dropped the rope. The eagle dropped down, down, down.

Alone on the other side, Glouskabi said, "Now I can go fishing."

Harcourt Brace School Publishers

TAKE-HOME BOOK

Dancing Colors

by *Allan Michael Cornell*

HARCOURT BRACE & COMPANY

It was time to do the last thing on Andrew's list. It was time to fix the broken window.

Andrew helped Jane make the paper patterns. He skillfully cut the new glass and removed the old, broken pieces. Then he put in new stained glass.

Andrew was busy soldering when he turned to his helper and said, "Get ready to cement!"

Jane pointed to herself and raised her eyebrows. "Me?" she asked.

"Yes, of course," answered Andrew. "You broke it, didn't you? Besides, I think you will be a good stained-glass artist one day."

Jane smiled and went right to work.

12

Andrew sat at his kitchen table, writing a list. It was still dark out, but he wanted to get an early start. It would be a busy day.

Andrew had been a "glass artist" for many years. He made colorful stained-glass windows. He not only made new windows but also fixed old, broken ones.

I need to write a list, so that I won't forget all I have to do today, he thought. *Without a list, I may omit something important.*

1

THINGS TO DO TODAY

1. Talk with the Johnsons.

2. Meet James.

3. Finish Dr. Crawford's stained-glass window.

4. Fix broken window.

The Johnsons want a new stained-glass window for their house, thought Andrew. *Well, a new project always stimulates my mind. No wonder I woke up so early!*

After that meeting, Andrew would have to hurry back to finish Dr. Crawford's window. Dr. Crawford was a dentist. She wanted a special stained-glass window. It would show a smiling face with straight, white teeth. She planned to put the window in her office.

2

apart. Before I solder, I brush *flux* onto the lead. Flux cleans the lead, so the solder will stick."

Jane watched Andrew work. Bit by bit, the glass picture came into being.

Then Andrew brushed a putty-like glue called *cement* into the lead.

"Cement helps hold the glass tightly in place," said Andrew. It makes the window stronger."

Finally, he held up the finished window.

"I hope Dr. Crawford likes it," he said.

"She will! She will!" said Jane happily.

11

Harcourt Brace School Publishers

Then Jane watched as Andrew fitted a cut piece of glass into a strip of lead.

"Lead *came* [kam] is the strip of soft metal that holds one piece of glass to another," Andrew told her. "We wear gloves to protect our hands. Lead can make people sick. After all the glass and lead came is together, I'll flux and solder the window."

"What does that mean?" Jane asked.

"*Solder*," Andrew said, "rhymes with 'fodder'." Solder is a mix of tin and lead. When solder is melted, it is VERY hot. I put melted solder wherever lead joins lead. This keeps the window from pulling

10

Next, Andrew would fix the broken window in his studio. A new newspaper carrier had thrown Andrew's morning paper right through it a couple of days ago. The carrier, James, had called to say he was sorry. He offered to pay for the window. Andrew invited James to help him fix it instead.

As they talked, Andrew could tell that James was excited about helping out. Since James seemed happy to learn, Andrew felt happy to teach him about glass work.

You never know, said Andrew. *Wouldn't it be nice if James turned out be a talented young glass artist? One of those prodigies?*

3

Andrew was ready to leave for the Johnsons'
house. But he couldn't find the plans he wanted to
show them.

"Where did I put them?" he asked himself.

They weren't on his work table. He was starting
to get nervous. The window plans had taken hours
to paint. Andrew had done them in watercolors. He
thought they looked beautiful.

"Ah," said Andrew. He had finally found the
plans in a cardboard tube near his coat.

4

"The glass has to be cut to the right size," said
Andrew. "If not, the finished piece won't fit the
window frame."

Jane smiled as she watched Andrew work.
Andrew thought Jane had listened very carefully to
what he had told her. She was happy when he said,
"Would you like to try cutting a piece of glass?"

Jane put on safety gear. She wore gloves,
goggles, and a mask. Then she picked up the glass
cutter.

"Be careful!" Andrew warned. Jane cut her first
piece of glass.

It was a perfect cut.

9

Andrew showed Jane a sketch. He explained that each of his windows started as a sketch—a simple drawing of his idea. Then he told her the steps. First, he used a projector to enlarge the sketch to the size of the window. Next he drew the shapes of the glass pieces on the big sketch. This was how he made his pattern for cutting the glass.

Jane loved the glass. Her head was filled with impressions of beautiful colors and light. She enjoyed watching Andrew cut the glass to the right shape and size.

8

The Johnson family had first seen Andrew's work at a local art exhibition. They liked the windows of his desert scenes best. Andrew told them that he had once lived in the Arizona desert. It had been an inspiration for his work.

This morning the Johnsons were excited to see Andrew's plan for their window.

"This window will look great in our home!" said Mrs. Johnson.

Andrew showed the Johnsons some glass samples. He helped them choose the glass for their new window.

"I can't wait to get started," he said as he waved good-bye.

5

As Andrew pulled his van into the driveway, he saw someone ringing his doorbell.

"You must be James," shouted Andrew. "Are you ready to work?"

"I'm ready to work. But my name is not James. It's Jane," said the girl. "You know my parents, the Andersons."

Andrew was surprised. But his workshop had noisy fans for cleaning the air as he worked. Sometimes he forgot to turn them off when he was on the phone. That was why he hadn't heard Jane clearly. "Sorry for the mix-up!" he told her. "Well, come on in!"

6

Andrew let Jane come into the workshop. Then he showed her his tools.

"Here is all the glass," he explained. "I keep pieces of the same color together."

Andrew held several pieces of his glass up to the light. It looked as if colors were dancing on the wall behind them. The effects were wonderful.

Jane learned that orange and red are called warm colors. Blue is a cool color.

"You probably don't use much blue in a sunny desert scene," said Jane.

Andrew smiled and nodded, "You're getting the idea!" he said.

7

TAKE-HOME BOOK

The Big Teacup
A Chinese Tale
*retold by **Meish Goldish***

HARCOURT BRACE & COMPANY

How much do you know about pottery?

Do you think each statement below is true or false?

(Answers are at the bottom of the page.)

1. The word *pottery* comes from the word *pot*.

2. Pottery is made of baked clay.

3. People in Egypt made the first pottery.

4. The ancient Chinese had a special way of making pottery that they kept a secret.

5. Today, making pottery is a popular hobby.

6. Putting pottery in a kiln makes it strong.

Answers: All the statements are true.

From the
Library
of

_____

As with many legends, this one ends happily. Yu Po and his family were now rich.

But what of Sun Ming?

Well, he still had his gold and the rest of his pottery. Even so, he was angry for a long, long time.

The villagers tried to cheer him up. They stood outside his big house. They called out:

"Sun Ming! Don't be sad that your big teacup died. Perhaps one day, your tiny teacups will give you grandchildren!"

Long ago in China, there was a poor man. His name was Yu Po. He and his family lived in a small village.

Yu Po was a potter. Potters were important in Chinese culture. Even so, Yu Po did not make much money. His life was not easy.

Each day, Yu Po sat at his work table. There he shaped beautiful cups, bowls, and plates. Everyone liked his work. But few could pay a good price for it. You see, nearly all the villagers were poor—except for Sun Ming.

Sun Ming was the richest person in the whole village. He had piles of gold. He also had a cupboard full of pottery… pottery that was worth quite a lot.

But Sun Ming was very selfish. He never shared his riches with anyone. He never even let people inside his house. Instead, he sat alone all day, counting his gold and his pottery.

Sometimes beggars came to Sun Ming's door. They would ask for a coin to buy some bread.

"Get away from my home!" Sun Ming would shout. The beggars always went away quickly.

Sun Ming lifted Yu Po off the ground.

"I will take you to the village judge!" he cried. "She will make you pay *much money*!"

Sun Ming dragged the potter through the streets. Yu Po cried loudly. Other villagers heard the noise and followed along.

Finally they reached the judge's house. The men went inside. They told their story to the judge.

The judge sat quietly. Then she said, "Sun Ming, Yu Po does not owe you anything."

"But why, your honor?" the rich man cried.

"You were foolish to believe that your cup had babies," said the judge. "So now you must be foolish again and believe your cup has died!"

That evening, Yu Po walked to Sun Ming's house again. The rich man was waiting outside.

"Yu Po," asked Sun Ming, "where is my big, beautiful teacup?"

Yu Po looked very sad. He began to cry.

"Oh, Sun Ming!" he sobbed. "This is so sad. Last night your teacup got sick and died!"

Sun Ming's face turned red. He grabbed Yu Po by the shirt.

"What do you mean?!" the rich man shouted. "A teacup cannot die! Give it back to me!"

"I cannot," cried Yu Po. "It is dead! I had to bury it!"

10

Day after day, Yu Po sat at his work table. As he worked, he thought. He thought about how poor he was. He also thought about how rich Sun Ming was.

One day, the poor potter had an idea. He knew how he would become rich!

That evening, after work, Yu Po walked to Sun Ming's house. As usual, the rich man was counting his gold coins. He heard a knock on the door.

"Who's there?" Sun Ming cried.

"It's Yu Po," the potter said.

"Go away!" the rich man shouted. "I'm not giving away any money!"

"I am not here for money," Yu Po said.

"Well, I don't wish to buy any pottery either," Sun Ming shouted. "Go away!"

"I am not here to sell," said Yu Po.

Sun Ming opened the door a crack.

"Then why are you here?" he asked.

3

Yu Po smiled. "A guest is coming to my home tomorrow," he said. "I want to serve him tea in a fine cup. But I have none. I hear that you own a big, beautiful teacup. Would you lend it to me?"

Sun Ming laughed. "Lend you my fine teacup? No!" He began to shut the door.

"I promise to take good care of it," Yu Po begged, "I will pay much money if it is harmed."

Sun Ming heard the words "much money." "You may borrow my fine teacup," he said. "But you must return it tomorrow night. Or you will pay *much money*!"

Yu Po took the big, beautiful cup home.

4

The next day, Yu Po did not go to work. Instead, he placed Sun Ming's big cup in a sack and walked to the city. He went straight to the pottery shop. Yu Po showed the cup to the shop owner.

"What a big, beautiful cup that is!" cried the owner. "I can see that it is very old. Very valuable!"

"Would you like to buy it?" asked Yu Po.

"Of course!" said the owner. "I will give you ten gold pieces for it!" And so she did.

Yu Po went home with the money. His wife couldn't believe her eyes.

"Where did you get such money?" she cried.

"My plan is working!" Yu Po said.

9

The next night, Yu Po returned to Sun Ming's house. He knocked on the door and said, "It's Yu Po."

Immediately, Sun Ming ran to greet him.

"Ah, my dear friend," Sun Ming smiled. "Welcome to my home! Would you like to borrow my big, beautiful teacup again?"

"Yes, please." Yu Po smiled.

Sun Ming was very excited. Perhaps his cup would have more babies at Yu Po's house. They would be worth a lot of money.

"Please! Take it! Take the cup," Sun Ming said.

The potter took the big, beautiful teacup and went home.

8

The next day, Yu Po woke up very early. He placed the beautiful cup on his work table. He looked at it for a long time. It was pale green. A traditional Chinese dragon was painted on the cup.

At last, Yu Po went to work. He searched the large tin cylinders that held his tools. He chose a knife and a small chisel. Then he took some white clay and began to shape it.

Yu Po made a tiny, green teacup. It looked just like Sun Ming's cup, only smaller.

Then Yu Po made two more tiny cups, just like the first. He painted dragons, just like the dragon on the large cup. Finally, he baked the cups in the kiln.

5

At last the cups were ready. Yu Po wrapped each one and put it in a sack. He put Sun Ming's large teacup in the sack, too.

No guest ever arrived at the potter's home for tea that day. You see, this was all part of Yu Po's plan to get rich!

That night, Yu Po took the sack to Sun Ming's house. The rich man was already waiting outside.

"I have your big, beautiful teacup," Yu Po said. He took it from the sack and handed it to Sun Ming. The rich man looked carefully at the cup in the moonlight.

"Good," Sun Ming sighed. "Now, go away!"

"Wait," Yu Po said. "I have some good news. It may sound odd. But in my home last night, your teacup had babies!"

"Babies?" Sun Ming frowned. "That *is* odd!"

Quickly, Yu Po reached into his bag. He pulled out the three tiny cups he had made. He gave them to Sun Ming. The rich man could see how special they were. They would look fine in his pottery cupboard.

"Sun Ming," Yu Po said, "you own the big teacup. You should have its babies, too."

Sun Ming wanted the three tiny cups very much. So he thanked Yu Po and carried them inside.

The first part of Yu Po's plan was done!

TAKE-HOME BOOK

Starting Over

by Allan Michael Cornell

HARCOURT BRACE & COMPANY

Harcourt Brace School Publishers

Every once in a while, Jonathan still thinks of Mike. He remembers how, in the old days, they rescued each other from alligators and bears. He has now even begun writing the adventures down. He has a new dream—to write a book. And on the first page of the book it will say, "To Mike, who helped me start over."

Jonathan Edwin was not like the other kids in his class. At least that's what Jonathan thought. He felt lonely a lot of the time. But that was all right. He was the new kid in school. If nobody paid attention to him, nobody could make fun of him either.

I hate starting over, he thought.

You see, Jonathan had started over many times.

Jonathan's mother worked for a big company that moved her from city to city. Jonathan was tired of moving. He was more than tired of moving.

"Three different houses in three different cities in the last four years!" he told her. "That's too many moves!"

Watching some kids play catch, Jonathan felt lonelier than ever.

Then he had an idea.

How about a new friend who already knows me? he thought. *That's it. I'll make up a friend. He'll just be in my own head. But at least he'll always be there wherever I have to go.*

I keep telling you great jokes, Jonathan continued. *But you never tell me any jokes of your own.*

Jonathan looked serious now. He took a deep breath. Then he said what he really wanted to say.

Mike, it's time for you to go away. I think I am ready for a real friend.

That very day, Jonathan went over to those kids who had waved at him. They shot baskets, flew a model airplane, and talked about their favorite books. They also traded phone numbers.

2

11

But Jonathan was beginning to have doubts about his good idea.

Mike, we've been friends for almost three weeks, he thought one day. *And you do everything I ask you to do. You go everywhere I ask you to go. You never argue with me. You never try to hurt my feelings. And you rescue me every time. Every time that I don't rescue you, that is.*

Jonathan could see Mike nod.

10

"Now I will start out in a new house and a new school with a new best friend—a made-up friend." Jonathan said out loud. "We'll do everything together!"

Suddenly, Jonathan heard something rustle.

He looked around, nervously. A squirrel was digging around for acorns in a pile of dry leaves. Jonathan sighed with relief. No one had heard, and no one would tease him. Some kids would think that nine was too old to have an imaginary friend. In a way, he did too. It's just that he was scared. Every time he made a friend, he had to give him up when it was time to move.

3

From then on, Jonathan was extra careful to keep his made-up friend a secret from everyone. But he kept on thinking about him.

He'll need a name, thought Jonathan. *I'll call him Mike.*

Jonathan liked the sound of "Mike." It sounded much stronger than "Jonathan."

One day Jonathan thought he saw a lion in the park. It was hiding under a bush and watching some kids from his class. Before Jonathan could even warn them, there was Mike! He swung from limb to limb. Then he dropped a big net on the lion. The Mayor gave them both a medal. They were on the evening news, too.

It was a great rescue! Jonathan felt really sorry he couldn't tell the kids all about how their lives had been saved.

In fact, Jonathan was a hero to Mike on many adventures. That is, when Mike wasn't being a hero to Jonathan.

Once Mike climbed a mountain to save Jonathan from an angry grizzly bear.

The next day Mike helped his friend out of a swamp. The water rippled with very hungry alligators.

Another time Mike pulled Jonathan out of a raging river.

I like our adventures, Jonathan said in his mind to Mike.

Mike seemed to agree.

8

When Jonathan got home from school that day, he felt great. He didn't feel alone anymore. He felt as if Mike was with him!

First he played basketball. Jonathan scored 42 points. He let Mike score 42 points, too.

Next he flew a model airplane. Jonathan threw the airplane with skill and style. Mike had the same skills.

Jonathan stopped to watch some kids playing in the park. The kids waved to Jonathan, but he ignored them. He already had a friend.

Jonathan had a great time that day. But he realized that he and Mike could do even more. They could share great adventures!

5

First, they hiked into a steamy rain forest. It was filled with huge trees and the calls of wild animals.

On this adventure, Jonathan had to rescue his buddy from the poisonous fangs of a giant snake. It was all coiled up on the ground, ready to attack. *Mike, you are very lucky to have such a brave friend as me,* thought Jonathan. He felt like a true hero.

Another day, Jonathan imagined he heard Mike yell for help. His new friend was pointing at something in the sky. Mike looked very scared. Jonathan looked up. A flying saucer! It was about to scoop Mike up. Jonathan whooped, ran, flapped his arms, and yelled at the same time. The saucer flew back into outer space.

TAKE-HOME BOOK

Maya Angelou: A Life of Words and Music

by Alice Cary

HARCOURT BRACE & COMPANY

From the

library of

The Amazing World of Maya Angelou

Maya Angelou was born on April 4, 1928. Her life has been so interesting that she has written five books about it. Here are some facts about this talented writer:

- Maya has traveled all over the world. She has lived in Egypt and Ghana. She speaks French, Spanish, Italian, Arabic, and Fanti, the language of Ghana.

- Maya's Inauguration Day poem is called "On the Pulse of Morning." It celebrates our country's history and people. A copy of the poem hangs in the White House.

On January 20, 1993, Maya was ready. She had finished the poem.

About noontime she stood beside President Clinton in Washington, D.C. Dressed in a dark coat with gold buttons, she looked dignified and graceful. She was surrounded by a sea of people waiting to hear her poetry.

She thought about Mrs. Flowers and her clear, strong voice. Maya took a deep breath. Then she shared her words with the world.

12

One January afternoon in 1993, people all over the world stopped to listen to a woman named Maya Angelou.

People who knew her as a girl would never have believed such a day would come. Back then, nobody listened to Maya.

1

Sometimes people forgot Maya was even there. She was a quiet girl. In fact, for several years, she stopped talking. She wouldn't talk to her mother or to her grandmother. She would only talk to her brother.

Because Maya didn't speak, some people thought she was stupid.

But her grandmother knew Maya was smart. She believed that someday Maya would have plenty to say.

2

part of the celebration when he took office.

Maya had won many awards. This, however, was her greatest honor.

She began to work on the poem. Every word had to be exactly right. Here was her chance to speak to the entire country.

Maya worked and worked. She wrote and rewrote. Sometimes she smiled. She knew everyone back in Stamps, Arkansas, would be listening on the big day. Black people. . . white people. . . people of every color!

11

Billie Holiday's words had come true. Maya Angelou was soon famous, but not for singing.

Once Maya had been a girl who said nothing. But all that had changed. Now, there was no stopping her.

She wrote plays, poetry, movie and TV scripts, and more books about her life. She gave hundreds of speeches.

In November 1992, Bill Clinton was elected President of the United States. A few weeks later he asked Maya to write a poem. She would read it as

Instead of speaking, Maya read as much as she could. And she listened. She listened to everyone who came into her grandmother's general store. She often heard things other people missed.

There was plenty to hear in Stamps, Arkansas, in the 1930s. Maya heard about segregation. She heard about all the things black people weren't allowed to do.

Maya didn't see many white people. Sometimes she thought they weren't real.

Maya loved to watch a woman named Bertha Flowers. She had smooth, black skin and wore beautiful dresses. She walked with grace and dignity.

One day Mrs. Flowers invited Maya to her house for cookies and lemonade.

"I understand you like books," Mrs. Flowers said. Maya nodded.

"It's not enough to read them," Mrs. Flowers said. "You have to read them *aloud.* Voices give words meaning."

Mrs. Flowers began to read aloud. Maya had never heard anyone read like this. Mrs. Flowers was turning words into poetry. Her voice sounded like music.

4

Maya decided she wanted to try to turn her own words into music. But she wouldn't sing. She would write.

She joined a writers' group in Harlem. The other writers in the group loved to hear Maya tell stories. They urged her to write the story of her life.

"When you speak, your words have rhythm," they told her. "Put that rhythm into your writing."

Maya did just that. Even the title of her book was about music. She called it *I Know Why the Caged Bird Sings.*

Many people thought the book showed that Maya was a genius.

9

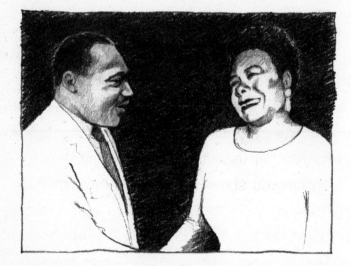

In New York City Maya heard Martin Luther King, Jr. give a speech.

Like Mrs. Flowers, this man knew how to turn words into music. Sometimes his voice was as soft as a bell. Then it roared like thunder. His message of freedom touched Maya's heart.

Maya wanted to help Reverend King. She put on a stage show called "Cabaret for Freedom." She hired black actors, singers, dancers and comedians. The show was filled with jubilation. It was a big hit!

Maya had changed a lot since she was a little girl. She began to speak up. She was proud of her heritage.

8

When Mrs. Flowers finished, she looked at Maya. "How do you like that?" she asked.

Maya knew she had to speak. She didn't want to disappoint Mrs. Flowers.

"Yes, ma'am," she mumbled.

Mrs. Flowers handed her a book.

"Memorize one of these poems," she said. "Next time you visit, I want you to recite for me."

Maya ran all the way home. She was thrilled. *Mrs. Flowers liked her. Mrs. Flowers thought she was special!*

The visit changed Maya. She began to talk again. She made new friends. She was the best student in her class.

In high school she studied drama and dance. She fell in love with theater and music.

5

Maya was a good student, but hard times were ahead. After she left school, she tried many different jobs. She didn't have much money. But she always had her dreams.

After a while, Maya's life seemed to take off like a rocket. She became a dancer. She learned choreography. Before long, she made her dance debut in Europe and in Africa.

She sang, too. She could sing almost any tempo and style. She sang folk, jazz, and blues.

6

One night a famous singer named Billie Holiday came to hear Maya sing.

Billie Holiday liked Maya. "You're going to be famous one day," she told Maya. "Really famous. But it won't be for singing."

Maya wanted to be famous. *How?* she wondered.

7